Lydgate's Minor Poems.

The Two Nightingale Poems.

BERLIN: ASHER & CO., 13, UNTER DEN LINDEN.
NEW YORK: C. SCRIBNER & CO.; LEYPOLDT & HOLT.
PHILADELPHIA: J. B. LIPPINCOTT & CO.

Lydgate's Minor Poems.

The Two Nightingale Poems.
(A.D. 1446.)

EDITED FROM THE MSS.
WITH INTRODUCTION, NOTES, AND GLOSSARY
BY
OTTO GLAUNING, Ph.D.

LONDON:
PUBLISHED FOR THE EARLY ENGLISH TEXT SOCIETY
By KEGAN PAUL, TRENCH, TRÜBNER & CO., LIMITED,
PATERNOSTER HOUSE, CHARING-CROSS ROAD.

OXFORD

UNIVERSITY PRESS

Great Clarendon Street, Oxford OX2 6DP
United Kingdom

Oxford University Press is a department of the University of Oxford.
It furthers the University's objective of excellence in research, scholarship,
and education by publishing worldwide. Oxford is a registered trade mark of
Oxford University Press in the UK and in certain other countries

© The Early English Text Society 1900

The moral rights of the authors have been asserted

Database right Oxford University Press (maker)

First Edition published in 1900

All rights reserved. No part of this publication may be reproduced,
stored in a retrieval system, or transmitted, in any form or by any means,
without the prior permission in writing of Oxford University Press,
or as expressly permitted by law, or under terms agreed with the appropriate
reprographics rights organization. Enquiries concerning reproduction
outside the scope of the above should be sent to the Rights Department,
Oxford University Press, at the address above

You must not circulate this book in any other form
and you must impose this same condition on any acquirer

Published in the United States of America by Oxford University Press
198 Madison Avenue, New York, NY 10016, United States of America

British Library Cataloguing in Publication Data
Data available

Library of Congress Cataloging in Publication Data
Data available

Extra Series, 80

ISBN 978-0-85-991993-7

CONTENTS.

	PAGE
PREFACE	vii
INTRODUCTION:	
§ 1. THE TITLE	xi
§ 2. DESCRIPTION OF THE MSS.	xi
§ 3. GENEALOGY AND CRITICISM OF THE TEXTS ...	xvii
§ 4. THE METRE	xx
§ 5. THE LANGUAGE	xxvi
§ 6. THE AUTHORSHIP	xxxiv
§ 7. THE DATE	xxxvi
§ 8. THE SOURCES	xxxviii
§ 9. CONCLUDING REMARKS	xlvi
THE FIRST POEM: THE NIGHTINGALE	1
THE SECOND POEM: A SAYENGE OF THE NYGHTYNGALE	16
NOTES	29
LIST OF ABBREVIATIONS	77
GLOSSARY	79

Dedicated
TO MY PARENTS.

PREFACE.

ABOUT two generations ago the works of Lydgate were very little known even among scholars in Middle-English literature, and the monk of Bury had little credit as a poet.[1] To the late Professor Zupitza it is due that, in the second half of the nineteenth century, more attention has been paid to the study of Lydgate's life and works. About this first real period of Lydgate study, inaugurated by the editor of *Guy of Warwick,* Professor Schick gives us a concise account on pp. xii and xiii of the Introduction to his excellent edition of the *Temple of Glas.* This fundamental work itself stands at the end of this period; and in it, for the first time, nothing has been neglected which could give a vivid picture of Lydgate's life and works as a whole; and his qualities as a poet have found a more favourable judgment than before.

The edition of the *Temple of Glas* has therefore served, in a way, as a basis for all the following publications of works of Lydgate.

To give a brief account of the further progress made in the study of Lydgate, I include in the following list all the editions of works of the monk, published in this second period, as far as they have come to my knowledge:[2]

STEELE, Robert, Lydgate and Burgh's Secrees of old Philisoffres. A version of the 'Secreta Secretorum.' Edited from the Sloane MS. 2464, with Introduction, Notes, and Glossary. (Publications of the Early English Text Society, Extra Series, LXVI.) London, 1894.

---

[1] See Ritson's "this voluminous, prosaick, and driveling monk," and "in truth, and fact, these stupid and fatigueing productions, which by no means deserve the name of poetry, and their stil more stupid and disgusting author, who disgraces the name and patronage of his master Chaucer, are neither worth collecting (unless it be as typographical curiositys, or on account of the beautyful illuminations in some of his presentation-copys), nor even worthy of preservation: being only suitablely adapted '*ad ficum & piperem,*' and other more base and servile uses."—*Bibl. Poet.* (1802), p. 87, 88.

[2] Th. Arnold's publication of Lydgate's verses on Bury St. Edmunds was not accessible to me.

TRIGGS, Oscar Lovell, The Assembly of Gods: or The Accord of Reason and Sensuality in the Fear of Death by John Lydgate. Edited from the MSS. with Introduction, Notes, Index of Persons and Places, and Glossary. (Publications of the Early English Text Society, Extra Series, LXIX.) London, 1896.

KRAUSSER, Emil, Lydgate's Complaint of the Black Knight. Text mit Einleitung und Anmerkungen. Inaugural-Dissertation zur Erlangung der philosophischen Doctorwürde der philosophischen Fakultät der Universität Heidelberg. [Sonderabdruck aus Anglia, Bd. xix.] Halle a. S., 1896.

ROBINSON, Fred N., On two Manuscripts of Lydgate's Guy of Warwick. Studies and Notes in Philology and Literature, Vol. v. (Child Memorial Volume.) [Harvard University.] Boston, 1896, pp. 177-220.

SCHLEICH, Gustav, Lydgate's Fabula duorum mercatorum. Aus dem Nachlasse des Herrn Prof. Dr. I. Zupitza, Litt.D., nach sämtlichen Handschriften herausgegeben. (Quellen und Forschungen zur Sprach- und Culturgeschichte der germanischen Völker. LXXXIII.) Strassburg, 1897.

SKEAT, Walter W., Chaucerian and other pieces. Edited, from numerous manuscripts. Being a supplement to the Complete Works of Geoffrey Chaucer (Oxford, in six volumes, 1894). Oxford, 1897. [No. 8: The Complaint of the Black Knight.—No. 9: The Flour of Curtesye.—No. 10: A Balade; in Commendation of Our Lady.—No. 11: To my Soverain Lady.—No. 12: Ballad of Good Counsel.—No. 13: Beware of Doubleness.—No. 14: A Balade: Warning Men to beware of deceitful Women.—No. 15: Three Sayings.—No. 22: A Goodly Balade.—No. 23: Go forth, King.]

HAMMOND, Eleanor P., London Lickpenny in *Anglia*, xx (1898), p. 404 ff. Halle, 1898.

HAMMOND, Eleanor P., Lydgate's Mumming at Hertford in *Anglia*, xxii (1899), p. 364 ff. Halle, 1899.

FURNIVALL, F. J., The Pilgrimage of the Life of Man, Englisht by John Lydgate, A.D. 1426, from the French of Guillaume de Deguileville, A.D. 1335. Edited ... Parts I and II (Publications of the Early English Text Society, Extra Series, LXXVII, LXXXIII). London, 1899, 1900.[1]

DEGENHART, Max, Lydgate's Horse, Goose, and Sheep. Mit Einleit-

---

[1] Part II was not accessible to me.

ung und Anmerkungen herausgegeben. (Münchener Beiträge zur Romanischen und Englischen Philologie. Heft xix.) Erlangen und Leipzig, 1900.

BROTANEK, Rudolf, Die Englischen Maskenspiele. (Wiener Beiträge zur Englischen Philologie xv.) Wien, 1902.

With the exception of the Pilgrimage of the Life of Man, for the edition of which the students of Middle-English language and literature are infinitely obliged to the labour of Dr. Furnivall, the larger works of the monk still[1] have to wait for critical or even handy editions. Of some of the so-called Minor Poems some accurate editions have been published, as we have mentioned; for the rest the student has still to recur to the edition by Halliwell, which has now turned out to be insufficient for modern researches. Therefore I have not looked upon it as a superfluous task to undertake, with Dr. Furnivall's approbation, a new edition of Lydgate's Minor Poems in critical texts for the Early English Text Society, of which the present two poems are to be the first part.

The pleasant, if somewhat difficult task now remains to me to discharge, in this short space, a heavy weight of indebtedness for much kind help received in the course of my work, an agreeable duty, recalling, as it does, much pleasant intercourse not only with books, but with men.

I wish to express my gratitude to the authorities and attendants of the British Museum, the Bodleian, and the University Libraries in Cambridge and Leiden, and to the librarians of Corpus Christi College, Oxford, and Corpus Christi and Pembroke College, Cambridge, for having kindly given me access to their treasures. I also wish to thank very cordially Dr. Furnivall and Mr. Jenkinson for much help in my work, and especially for great personal kindness.

Dr. Furnivall, and Miss Annie F. Parker of Oxford, have been kind enough to oblige me very much by reading the proofs of the texts with the manuscripts.

In more than one respect I have to acknowledge my deep indebtedness to Professor Schick: not only do I thank him for his continued personal interest in this work, but also for his suggestive teaching; the influence of both will be noticed everywhere throughout the following pages.

[1] November 1901.

Munich, February 1902.

§ 1. *The Title.* § 2. *Description of the MSS.*

INTRODUCTION.

§ 1. THE TITLE.

THERE is but little to be said about the titles of our poems, as there are but slight differences to be stated. MS. c has the title: *The nightyngale,* supplied by a later hand; its running title is also: *The nyghtynghale.* As this running title is in the same handwriting as the poem itself, we may conclude that it is the original title. MS. C shows the title in a modern hand: *The Nightingale by Iohn Lidgate.* MS. H got its title from Stowe: it runs: *A sayenge of the nyghtyngale;* and in MS. A we find, again in the old chronicler's hand: *Here folowinge begynneth a sayenge of þe nightingalle Imagened and cumpyled by daune Iohn Lidgate, munke of Berye.*[1] Therefore the first poem may be christened: *The Nightingale,* the second: *A Sayenge of the Nyghtyngale.*

§ 2. DESCRIPTION OF THE MSS.

A. FIRST POEM.

1. *MS. Cotton Caligula A. II* = c.

London, British Museum; see *Catal. Cotton MSS.,* p. 42.[2] Compare also Furnivall, *Percy's Fol. MS.,* II, p. 411; Sarazin, *Octavian (Altenglische Bibliothek,* III), p. ix ff.; Kaluza, *Libeaus Desconnus (Altenglische Bibliothek,* V), p. ix; Gough, *On the Middle English Metrical Romance of Emare,* Kiel, 1900, p. 1 ff. Paper book in 4°; date: second half of the xvth cent. Kaluza, p. ix, says: " C. Cott. Calig. A. II, eine Papierhandschrift aus der Regierungszeit Heinrich's VI. Furnivall (*Percy's Fol. MS.,* II, p. 411) setzt sie in das Iahr 1460; sie gehört aber wohl noch in das 2. Viertel des 15. Iahrhunderts." I do not think that this statement quite hits the mark, and should prefer Dr. Furnivall's opinion. Our poem extends from fol. 59 a–64 a (formerly fol. 57 a–62 a);

[1] This reads like a copy of one of John Shirley's titles.
[2] There is a mistake in this catalogue: the Christian name of Hoveden is "Iohn," not "Sam." (*D. N. B.* xxvii, 427 a, ff.).

§ 2. Description of the MSS.

fol. 1–139 of the MS. are in one handwriting. The title, supplied by a later hand, is: *The nightyngale;* the running title on fol. 59 b, 60 b, 61 b, 62 b, 63 b the same, with slight variations in spelling; fol. 60 a, 62 a, 63 a, 64 a are without running title. On fol. 61 a the first line of that page (l. 155), with exception of the last word, is found once more on the top of the page in a very bad handwriting. The colophon runs: *Amen .;. Explicit.* With few exceptions, we find capitals at the beginnings of the lines, and they are illuminated in red. The stanzas are marked by a certain sign on the margin. In the index of the MS. we read: *Another poeme intitled the nightingall.*

The abbreviations are quite clear and in conformity with the common usage; the scribe only shows some inconsistency in using *n* with a curl. In Romance words[1] ending in *-on*, this curl is generally meant for *-oun*; as in derisioún 309, confusioún 311, consecracioún 405, sauacioún 406, that is to say, when the stress is laid on the ending. Then, the vowel is the same as in: doun 64, 80, 126, 276, 279, 290, 339, 395, soun 66, croun 312, where *n* with curl is always shown. If, however, the ending is unaccented, and the vowel therefore shortened, the scribe expresses the difference by writing: séson 22, 28, 35, 58, réson 24, 60, 117, 317, enchéson 61, párdon 228. This system is often violated; not only do we find lésoñ 39, lamentácioñ 163, pássioñ 328, compássioñ 372 with curled *n*, but the scribe also applies the overline in words where he is not authorized in the least to do it, as in doñ (p.p.) 148, 382, borñ 156, 313, thorñ 312, moñ 350. I have therefore expanded this abbreviation only in the first class of cases; in the rest I have marked it by a stroke above the $n = ñ$.

The scribe has very few peculiarities in his spelling, and the poem in general shows an orthography not very much differing from the standard of Chaucer's spelling. We find a predilection for *ll*,[2] not only in the Latin ending *-al*: mortall 77, morall 109, originall 142, celestyall 145, speciall 176, 327, etc., eternall 413;—but in other words too: sotell 136, appell 151, pepyll 152, purpull 310, Eysell 368. Other consonants are not generally found in doubled form, though we have always: myddes 99, 339, 340, etc. Instead of the original spirant we find the media in: Wheder 38, 127, oder 124, 291; de 19 may be due to the assimilating power of the

---

[1] Compare Schick, *T. G.*, p. lxi.
[2] See Morsbach, *Mittelenglische Grammatik*, p. 40, Anm. 2.

§ 2. Description of the MSS.

preceding *d*, or it is a mere carelessness of the scribe.—*y* occurs as a consonant, representing O.E. palatal ȝ, in: yaf 61, 389, Ayen 130, 226, 402, Yevyng 194, yate 325; prosthetic in "yerth" 123, 384, 395.—There are only a few cases where we find *i* (*y*) for *e* in endings:[1] hertis 21, 62, bemys 391; banyshid 383; wyntyr 27, aftir 92, 265, etc.; pepyll 152.—The scribe always writes: be (= by) 22, 23, 35, 39, etc.; whech 46, 88, 91, etc.; Thenk (60), 139, 153, etc.; besy 353.—*n* and *l* are not unfrequently omitted: conny[n]ge 112, begynny[n]g 121, wor[l]dly 132, 153, wor[l]de 162, etc.

2. MS. Corpus Christi College, Oxford, 203 = C.

Oxford, Library of Corpus Christi College; see Coxe, *Cat. Cod. MSS. in Coll. Aul. Oxon.* II. On vellum, small 8°; date: second half of the xvth century. Our poem begins on p. 1, ends on p. 21, and is written throughout by the same scribe, though it is not likely that the whole was finished at once. There is no title by the hand of the scribe, nor any running title. At the end stands: *Amen. Explicit.* The index at the beginning, in recent handwriting, has: *The Nightingale. By Iohn Lydgate. Ded. to the Duchesse of Buckingham i. e. Anne, daughter of Ralph Nevill first Earle of Westmerland, wife of Humfrey Stafford, created Duke of Buck.* 1444. (See § 7.) Below: *Proverbium Scogan*,[2] p. 22. *Proverbium R. Stockys*,[3] p. 23. *Ext. under Chaucers Name among his Workes*, f. 335. *b. b.* Middle of the page: *Henry Duke of Warwick, p.* 17. *dyed* 1446. At the bottom of the page: *Liber Collegii Corporis Christi Oxon Ex dono Gulielmi Fulman*[4] *A. M. hujus Collegii quondam Socii.* These last lines are of still later date.

There are no initials in the MS., and at the beginning of the lines capitals are generally used. On p. 1, which is badly injured by dirt, we find a Latin invocation of the Virgin Mary: *Assit principio sancta Maria meo. Amen.* Then follows a short prose treatise, in which the contents of the poem are given by the scribe, as I think, not by Lydgate himself, judging from its incorrectness (compare § 8). At the beginning an initial was to be inserted, probably by the hand of the illuminator, but was forgotten afterwards. The introduction and the first two stanzas are, in our

---

[1] See Schick, *T. G.*, p. lxv, note 3.
[2] See Ritson, *B. P.*, p. 97–98; *D. N. B.* li, p. 1; Kittredge in *Notes and Studies in Philology and Literature* 1. (Harvard University) Boston, 1892, p. 109 ff.
[3] See Ritson, *B. P.*, p. 106. [4] See *D. N. B.* xx, p. 326 ff.

§ 2. Description of the MSS.

edition, taken from this MS., as they are not found in MS. c. But from st. 3 onwards, the Caligula MS. has been preferred as basis (see § 3).—ll. 299 and 300 are transposed in this MS. In l. 335 "hen(ne)," l. 336 the *e* of "whenn(e)" is cut down in binding, and l. 399 "shede" is illegible.

Some of the most conspicuous orthographic and phonetic peculiarities of the scribe are the following. The voiceless *s* is given as *ss*: Assendyth iv, gesse 86, blessyd 259, or *sc*: sentensce 12, sensce 16, Ascendyng 26, or *c*: secyth 37, or *s*: persed 52, perse 138, conseyte 60 (Schleich, *Fabula*, p. liii). About 'noresynge' 30, compare ten Brink, § 112; about 'sclepe' 29, 35, 44, etc. (but 'slepe' 118), 'sclowth' 57, 'scle' 161, etc., compare Varnhagen in *Anglia, Anzeiger*, vii (1884), p. 86–91.—*w* often occurs as a second constituent in diphthongs (?), representing O.E. *ú* or O.Fr. *ū*: trowblos 48, owre (= hour) 78, 86, (= our) 264, Abowte 105, fownde 108, nowmbere 125, downe 126, etc.—Compare: sclowth 57, trowth 374; revth 344; ruthe 372.—Twice, *w* is put instead of *v*: Awayll 76, concewe 134.—*c* occurs for *g* in: can 25, 136, 308, canne 54, neclygence 65.—þ occurs in: þu 156, þat 394.—*y* as a consonant, representing O.E. palatal 3, in: yaf 61, 389, yeuynge 194, Ayene 226, 402; prosthetic in: yerth 348, 384, 395, yeke 402.

The scribe shows a great predilection for putting *i* or *y* for *e* in endings: myddys viii, ourys xi; declaryd 17, secyth 37, boryn 156, etc.; lityll 1, wyntyre 27, Whedyre 38, opyn 100, etc. Besides we find: this (= thus) 28, 178, thys 169, ych (= each) 143 (vche 236), fynde (= fiend) 353, thyñ (= then) 388. Less frequently than *i* or *y* we find *u* in endings instead of *e*: murthus 74, clowdus 94, bemus 391; owuthe 116; vndurstondeñ xii, ffadure xiii, remembure 119, Appull 151, pepull 152. In some cases a special flourish is used for abbreviating the ending -*us*, as in galantus 11, hertus 21, 62, kalendus 45, boffettus 255.—hure i, ii, iv, 5, 6, 39, hur 4, etc., but hyre 7, 10, hyr 8, 9, etc.—*e* for *i*: *a.*, in unaccented syllables: mescheue 137, orygenall 142, rightwesnesse 204, consydrenge 234; yef 177, yeff 196, hes (= his) 410; *b.*, in accentuated syllables: leue 168, 384, leueste 172. 'perseue' 67, 'conceuede' 68, 'concewe' 134 on one side, and 'deceyve' 136 on the other are no peculiarities of the scribe, but the representatives of the O.Fr. double forms: 'concevóns': stress on the ending, and 'concéif': stress on the stem.

As in MS. c, the scribe fairly often has a flourish above *n*. A glance at the following examples will justify my reproducing it as in

§ 2. *Description of the MSS.*

MS. c: swañ iii, dou*n* viii, crystyñ x, passyou*n* xi, vndurstondeñ xii, mañ xiv, Ascencyone xviii, etc.

Moreover, we find that the scribe sometimes omits single letters: lame[n]table v, An[d] x, 155, 349, rygh[t] 59, Rygh[t] 63, etc., ffe[r]thyre 85, wor[l]de 121, etc.

B. SECOND POEM.

1. *MS. Harleian* 2251 = *H*.

London, British Museum; see *Catal. MSS. Harl.*, II, p. 578, 581, and 582. A paper book in small fol.; Foerster, *Herrig's Archiv*, ciii, p. 149 ff., dates it 1459, from internal evidence. This MS. was always[1] considered to be written by Shirley's hand, till Foerster in the article mentioned above proved that this opinion was erroneous. Our poem, in one handwriting, is found on fol. 229 *a*–234 *b* (formerly fol. 255 *a*–260 *b*). The title, in the hand of Stowe, the historian, runs: *A sayenge of the nyghtyngale*. No running title. At the end we read: *Of this Balade Dan Iohñ Lydgate made nomore.*— At the beginning, there is an initial in red and blue; the headings of the lines generally begin with capitals, which are illuminated with red. There is no index in the MS.—l. 236 is omitted.

There are dots marking the cæsural pause. I think they teach us nothing, as they are put in very arbitrarily by the scribe—*e. g.* l. 8 after: forsoth, l. 9: song, l. 31: hem, l. 36: herde, l. 87: doo, l. 97: dide, l. 218: me,—so I do not reproduce them or take them into consideration when dealing with the metre.

Of the peculiarities of Shirley (see above and § 3), mentioned by Furnivall, *Odd Texts*, p. 78, and Schick, *T. G.*, p. xxiii, we find here but: *uw* for *ew*: -huwed 2, nuwe 15, suwen 163.—Other peculiarities of the scribe are: *i* (*y*) for *e* in endings: fowlis 4, sterris 38, grassis 39, briddis 55, 59, 64, handis 114; meanyth 56, 82, takith 65, 83, Betokenyth 66, Shakith 74, qwakyth 74; callid 25, 333, blessyd 127, 143, 249, 364, pressid 154, offendid 213; gardyn 53, 340, etc.; also: hym (= hem) 117, 282, etc.—*ie* for *e* (Schleich, *Fabula*, p. xxxv) occurs in: bien 17, 29, 106, 362, cliere 36, 252, 284, 362, chiere 46, fieble 186; triewe 69 (17, 56, 80).—*w* as a vowel (Schleich, *Fabula*, p. xlv): twnes 36, 58, etc.; as the second element of a diphthong in: Emerawdes 34.—Very

---

[1] *e. g. Cat. Harl. MSS.* II, p. 578; Morley, *English Writers*, v, p. 148 note; Skeat, *Chaucer*, I, p. 57; D. N. B. lii, p. 134*a*; Steele, *Secrees*, p. xi; Schleich, *Fabula*, p. I.

xvi   § 2. *Description of the MSS.*

often consonants appear in doubled form: bridde 20, 51, 71, langwisshyng 29,[1] Cherissh 30,[1] Castell 32, allone 48, 160, etc.

2. *Additional MS.* 29729 = *A.*

London, British Museum; see *Catal. Addit. MSS.* On paper, small fol., in the handwriting of Stowe; date 1558 (see Catal. Index). Our poem extends from fol. 161 *a*–166 *a*. The title runs: *Here folowinge begynneth a sayenge of þe nightingalle Imagened and cumpyled by daune Iohn Lidgate, munke of Berye.* There are no running title, no colophon, no initials; capitals are also rare and without system. On the title-page of the MS. we read: *Daune Lidigate monke of Burye, his Woorkes,* supplied below, by a later hand: *written by Stowe.*

According to fol. 179 *a* of the MS. (compare also Schick, *T. G.*, p. xix), the MS. is a copy by Stowe from Shirley, therefore we are not surprised to find some cases where the peculiarities of the original spelling are preserved (see Schick, *T. G.*, p. xxiii): *uw* for *ew*: -huwed 2, truwe 30, 69, huwe 121.—*e*- for *y*- in the p.p. in: eblent 130, emeynt 137, elefft 220.—There are many examples which still show Shirley's predilection for *ff* (see p. xii[2]), though it is possible that these may be due to the same predilection of Stowe's, as we find an exceedingly large number of cases where other consonants too (see below) are doubled without any apparent reason: *ff* in: sauffe 10, yff 50, 77, 207, theffe 102, lifft 103, cheffe 246, 251, etc., off 252, 312, soffte 264, lyffe 342, contemplatiffe 343.

Other peculiarities are: *i* or *y* in endings for *e*: grasys 39, thevys 174; pressin 152, pressyd 154, forsakyne 170, spokyn 202, bonchyd 206, -percyd 210, blessyd 249, clepyd 257, makid 298; gardin (gardyn) 53, 340, etc.—Notice: pardy 24, maundy 248.— *a* for *e* before *r*: evar 159, 178, nevar 172, 179.—*w* as a vowel, occurs in: nwe 123, (but newe 15), endwre 181, wnkynd 182; emerawdes 34.—Not without interest for the date of the MS. is the changing of *d* and *th* in the words: moder 162, mother 257, fader 259, fathers 274, and also the forms of the pronouns (see § 5).— Of the doubled consonants, *ll* occurs in the largest number of examples: dalle 9, nightingalle 11, allone 48, -sellfe 72, etc., chaundellabre 320, mortall 352, crystall 362, etc.—*tt* in: grett 67, 88, etc., fett 114, 283, Pylatt 138, -outten 179, etc.—The pron. possess. fem. occurs as: her 13, 36, hur 15, 16, 23, hir 37, 62, 73, hyr 83,

---

[1] See Schleich, *Fabula,* p. li; ten Brink, § 112 *a*.

etc.—Compare: eghen 108, egghen 130, eghe 177, eyen 194.—
Obvious mistakes are seen in: dedemcyon (for: redemcyon) 284,
assay[l]e 308; about 'chayne' (?) 318, compare the note to that
line.

§ 3. GENEALOGY AND CRITICISM OF THE TEXTS.
I. *The MSS. c and C.*

The text of the first poem is handed down to us in fairly good
condition, as the two MSS. do not generally differ much from each
other, so that we may say with certainty that both go back to a
common original. But notwithstanding the general coincidence,
they cannot either of them have been derived directly from the
other:

1. c cannot be derived from C, because, though there is no very
remarkable difference in the date, c is certainly the elder of the two,
and, moreover, C has a very long list of its own individual faults,
where c has the better reading:

40. mervell c] merevell hit C.—42. mery] *om.*—71. is] *om.*—
81. endure shall] enduryth.—90. song] schange.—95. enlumyned]
enlewmyde.—106. of] to.—115. cristen-man] kyrsteñ manes.—128.
fall] schall.—129. the] the rygh.—139. thi-self] they-selfe.—165.
With] With the.—166. byddeth the] by the.—173. these] this.—
202. age] *om.*—212. Noght] How.—236. vn-to] in-to.—277. syng-
yng] syngnified.—280. in] *om.*—299, 300] *transposed in C.*—302.
youre] oure.—314. Vnto] Vpoñ.—323. Ye] The.—331. peple] pepull
that.—333. hym to] to hym.—369. crym] tyme.—385. all] Allso.

2. C is independent of c, because the first two stanzas are missing
in c. The prose treatise at the beginning in C, being not by the
poet, but probably by the scribe (see § 8), may be a special foreword
to C, and independent of the form in which the poem may have
circulated. Farther, though the scribe of C is not a very careful
man, C offers in some cases the preferable reading, where c is wrong,
though it is not at all likely that the careless scribe of C corrected
these errors:

130. quert C] quarte c.—150. Anone] or none.—222. Ley] Ley
that.—233. aswaged was] was aswaged.—243. redy is] ys redy the.—
257. of] of pite &.—270. Restreyne] Restreyned.—283. To] The.—
314. peynes] peynes, calde.—339. avale] a-vaile.—348. in] in a.—
374. all] *om.*

xviii § 3. *Genealogy and Criticism of the Texts.*

We hence conclude that c and C go back to a common original MS. X, which is lost, but probably through the medium òf a MS. Z. As arguments, we can bring forward that, roughly speaking, both versions exhibit the same wording, and that some peculiarities in spelling—e. g. *i* (*y*) for *e* in endings—are found in both MSS. in the same places. Considering that c has mostly the better reading, we may even be allowed to suppose that C is not a direct copy from MS. Z, but from an intermediate MS. Y which has also been lost.

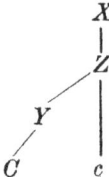

II. *The MSS. H and A.*

The case here is very much the same as in the foregoing paragraph. The nearly complete parallelism of the text, which on the whole is well preserved, forces us to assume a common original; the more, when we consider that certain more or less delicate traces of the peculiarities in the original spelling are preserved in both MSS. But here also the two MSS. are independent of each other.

1. H cannot be derived from A, because it is just a hundred years older than the other. Besides, A shows a certain number of individual readings, which are not found in H.

2. westward H] estwarde A.—6. taught[e]] taught tho.—20. sle] sleth.—23. theyr] hur.—30. affectiouñ] affectyons.—43. that] *om.*—58. herdest] haddest.—63. to encres] tencresse them.—65. the] *om.*—115. in] of.—118. an] *om.*—131. and] and to.—155. is] is I.—165. diden flee] dyd wend.—230. grete] *om.*—273. rayle] ryall.—281. kyndenesses] kyndnes.—282. the[e]] *om.*—284. a] *om.*—295. palme] pallis.—299. key] kepe.—318. Tau] chayne.—329. thurgh] ouer.—354. Callyng] called.—362. thaleys] paleys.

3. Nor can A come from H: the peculiarities of Shirley's spelling are better preserved in A than in H; l. 236 is omitted in H; further A sometimes has the better reading than H.

4. in A] *om.* H.—62. fyry] fayre.—103. and] at.—144. can] *om.*—153. and] and the.—202. heringe of tales] tales heryng.—224. them] *om.*—232. heued] *om.*—236. *om.* H.—302. ascencyon]

§ 3. *Genealogy and Criticism of the Texts.*

Redempcioun.—313. whoo] *om.*—344. For] ffrom.—346. Is] It is.—351. þat] *om.*

It is impossible to believe that A in these cases should have, of itself, found the true reading, considering the long list of inferiorities above, where A always ranks secondarily to H. At last, two in themselves insignificant faults of A seem to me very interesting. l. 334 A writes: palegorye, whereas H has: the Allegorye; again, in l. 362 A: paleys, H thaleys. I think it is evident that Stowe would not have misread H, but he must have had a MS. before him, where the old þ was used: now þ is one of Shirley's predilections.

III. *The MSS. taken as bases.*

The foregoing discussion of the genealogy of the MSS. has proved that, 1. in both cases we have not the original; 2. in each case which of the MSS. is preferable: In c and H the number of better readings outweighs the faults; moreover, both are older than C and A, so I took them as the bases of my texts.

The introduction and the first two stanzas of the c-version are taken from C, not being found in c. I need not say that I profited by C and A to correct the errors of c and H.

Every deviation from the MSS. taken as bases is indicated. Square brackets are used to supply omissions of words, syllables, and letters. Where it was not possible to use brackets, I marked the altered word, or the first of a group of words, by an asterisk. In all cases the reading of c or H is each time noted at the bottom of the page. Abbreviations are expanded in the usual way (italics); about ñ compare § 2; underlined proper names in H are printed in heavy type. Various readings of C and A, so far as they represent variations of meaning, are given at the bottom of the page. Mere orthographical or phonetic variations of no interest are neglected, the peculiarities of the scribes being discussed at large in § 2. About the cæsural pause, compare Description of MS. H, p. xv above. The tags to d, f, g, r are not printed.

The entire punctuation is mine.—*ff*, at the beginning of the lines, is replaced by *F*. As it is often very difficult to say whether the letter standing in the MS. is a capital or not, I have introduced capitals regularly at the beginning of a line, and in proper names. The indefinite article, certain adverbs, or other short words are often joined to the word following them; these I have separated. On the contrary, words separated by the scribe are joined by hyphens.

§ 4. THE METRE.

"*In many cases it is, however, impossible to classify a line* . . ."
Schick, *T. G.*, p. lix.

1. *Structure of the Verse.*

The metrical form of the poems is the Rhyme Royal (Schipper, *Englische Metrik*, I, § 196; Schick, *T. G.*, p. liv), seven-line stanzas of five-beat lines, with the sequence of rhymes *a b a b b c c*. In the first poem we find st. 34 with the sequence *a b a b b a c*; in the second one st. 18 and st. 54 are six-line stanzas with the rhymes *a b a b c c*; st. 20 is an eight-line stanza with *a b a b b b c c*.

Following Prof. Schick's system in his *T. G.*, p. lvii ff., we have five varieties of verse.

Type A. "*The regular type, presenting five iambics, to which, as to the other types, at the end an extra syllable may be added. There is usually a well-defined cæsura after the second foot, but not always.*"

I. *Poem.*

15. Commándyng theým // to hére wyth téndernésse
17. Whos sónge and déth // declåred ís exprésse
19. But nóthelés // consídred thé senténce
21. And fléschly lúst // out óf theyre hértis cháce
23. In príme-téns // renóueled yére be yére
40. Gret mérvell ís // the endúryng óf hir thróte.

Of such entirely regular lines we have 133. Besides, I read as of type A 98 lines where the *-e* in the cæsura was surely dropped in Lydgate's time, especially before vowels; compare Krausser, *Complaint*, p. 14, and O. Bischoff, *Englische Studien*, xxv, p. 339:

8. Vn-tó the týme // hyr ládylý goodnésse
9. Luste fór to cáll // vn-tó hyr hígh presénce
41. That hér to hére // it ís a sécond héuen
49. But, ás god wóld, // in hást y wás Reléued
56. Me cálde ande saýde : // "A-wáke & Rýse, for sháme
67. For tó perceýue // with áll my díligénce.

In the following examples the cæsura presents a particular interest :

Usual cæsura after the arsis of the 1. measure : ll. 73, 297.[1]

Lyric cæsura after the thesis of the 3. measure : ll. 45, 46, 74, 108, 121, 129, etc. = 37 lines.

---

[1] For the usual cæsura after the arsis of the 2. measure : see the two classes of regular lines above.

§ 4. *The Metre.*

Usual cæsura after the arsis of the 3. measure: ll. 12, 16, 32, 60, 84, 86, etc. = 20 lines.

Lyric cæsura after the thesis of the 4. measure: ll. 53, 314, 341.

Without apparent cæsura: ll. 3, 47, 48, 52, 54, 57, etc. = 20 lines.

To sum up, we have in the first Poem 133 + 98 + 82 = 313 lines of type A, or 76·5 per cent. of all the lines.

II. *Poem.*

Entirely regular lines: 85 examples.

Regular lines with mute -e in the cæsura: 79 examples.

Usual cæsura after the 1. measure: l. 72.

Lyric cæsura after the thesis of the 2. measure: ll. 66, 106.

[Usual cæsura after the arsis of the 2. measure: all the regular lines.]

Lyric cæsura after the thesis of the 3. measure: ll. 1, 4, 6, 13, 17, etc. = 81 lines.

Usual cæsura after the arsis of the 3. measure: ll. 221, 286, 317, 351.

Without cæsura: ll. 68, 115, 177, 180.

Together 85 + 79 + 92 = 256 lines of the type A or 68 per cent.

Type B. "*Lines with the trochaic cæsura, built like the preceding, but with an extra-syllable before the cæsura.*"

I. *Poem.*

26. Phebùs ascéndyng, // clere schýnyng ín hys spére
28. And lústy séson // thus néwly réconcíled
35. Whych ín her séson // be slép[e] sét no tále
39. Redlỳ rehérsyng // her léson aỳ be róte
65. Expélling clérly // all wílfle négligénce
71. Ande ín Auróra, // that ís the mórowe gráy.

65 lines = 15·5 per cent.

The following 3 lines present special difficulties, wherefore I give them scanned:

[4. Thĕ Dŭchés ŏf Bókўnghăm,[1] // ănd ŏf hŭr ĕxcĕlléncĕ]
30. Vntó thĕ nŏrĭshĭng // ŏf éuerў crĕătŭrĕ[2]
251. Rĕmémbrўng spĕciăllў // v̆pón thĭs óure ŏf prímĕ.

---

[1] Compare Shakspere's Buckingham = Bucknam.
[2] Schleich, *Fabula*, l. 27; Krausser, *Complaint*, l. 59.

§ 4. *The Metre.*

II. *Poem:* 39 lines = 10 per cent.
Type C. "*The peculiarly Lydgatian type, in which the thesis is wanting in the caesura, so that two accented syllables clash together.*"

I. *Poem.*

31. With-oúte whéch // bráynes múst be mád
34. Meuèth to wách, // ás the nýghtingále
85. Till thát hyt drógh // fórther óf the dáy
122. Ande hów grete gód, // óf his éndles mýght
123. Hath héven ande yérth // fórmed wíth a thóght
127. Hýgh or lówe, // whéder-so-éuer thow bé.

21 lines = 5 per cent.

II. *Poem.* 44 lines = 12 per cent.

Compare the amount of this type in The Complaint of the Black Knight, 1402–3 = 10 per cent.
Temple of Glas, 1403 = 3·5 per cent.
Hors, Goose, and Sheep, 1436–40 = 6·2 per cent.
Nightingale, I. Poem, 1446 = 5 per cent.
Nightingale, II. Poem, ? = 12 per cent.

Type D. "*The acephalous or headless line, in which the first syllable has been cut off, thus leaving a monosyllabic first measure.*"

I. *Poem.*

22. Méued of Córage // be vértu óf the séson
24. Gládyng éuery hért // of véray réson
33. Excepte thoó // that kýndelý natúre
131. Sáue thy soúle, // or élles shált thou smérte
146. Críst, consýderyng // the grét captýuyté
254. Poúnce Pylát, // that Iúge was óf the láwe.

11 lines = 2·5 per cent.

With epic caesura (as in type B): 4 examples.
With usual caesura after the arsis of the 2. measure: 6 examples.
With usual caesura after the arsis of the 3. measure: l. 24.

II. *Poem.* 38 lines = 10 per cent.

With epic caesura (as in type B): 4 examples.
With usual caesura after the arsis of the 2. measure: 16 examples.
With lyric caesura after the thesis of the 3. measure: 18 examples.
Type E. "*Lines with a trisyllabic first measure.*"
Lines of this type occur but in the I. Poem 3 = 0·5 per cent.
4. See type B.
13. Of the nýghtyngále, // and ín there mýnde enbráce

§ 4. *The Metre.*

113. Be this nýghtingále, // thát thus fréshly cán.

The following list will show the proportion of the types in both poems:

	I. Poem.	II. Poem.
Type A	76·5 per cent.	68 per cent.
„ B	15·5 „	10 „
„ C	5 „	12 „
„ D	2·5 „	10 „
„ E	0·5 „	— „

The proportion of the different kinds of cæsuras is as follows:

	I. Poem.	II. Poem.
Usual cæsura	68 per cent.	60 per cent.
Epic „	17 „	12 „
Lyric „	10 „	27 „
Cæsura wanting	5 „	1 „

Compare Krausser, *Complaint*, p. 16, 17, and Degenhart, *Hors*, p. 35. Some lines exhibit the peculiarities of two types at the same time, as in the first poem l. 4 of B and E, l. 113 of C and E and l. 127 of C and D; in the second l. 83 also of C and D.

Inverted accent is found in the first poem in 29 lines (7 per cent.) and in the second in 37 lines (10 per cent.); again 24 (= 83 per cent.) of those 29 lines have it in their first measure, of the 37 lines of the second poem 25 or 70 per cent. have it at their very beginning. Double thesis may nearly always be read by slurring over without injuring the flow. The one line 251 of the first poem makes an exception, and perhaps ll. 195, 197: *Fro mórow to nýght* . . .

The absence of thesis I observed in ll. 38, 397 of the first poem.

Hiatus is very often found. In the c-version in 81 lines, in the H-version in 65 lines.

Synizesis, elision, syncope, etc. also occur very often in both poems. I only mention, as being of particular interest, ll. 137, 138 of the second poem: This is he . . . = This' he; comp. Schick, *T. G.*, p. lix; Krausser, *Complaint*, p. 15, l. 241.

Slight traces of alliterative traditions also occur in our poems (compare ten Brink, § 334 ff.; McClumpha, *The Alliteration of Chaucer*. Diss. Leipzig. 1888; Triggs, *Assembly*, p. xx; Krausser, *Complaint*, pp. 17, 18; Morrill, *Speculum Gy de Warewyke*, p. cxlvii). However, I rather doubt that any system is to be observed; only poetical formulas like the following ones may have been used by Lydgate more or less intentionally:

c: Redly rehersyng 39, melodiouse and mery 42, slombre-bed of slouth & sleep 57, my myrthes ande my melodye 74 (104), to hyrt then hele 154, vice ande vertu 214, bareyne ... and bare' 245, salf thy sore 319, woo or wele 320, soth to say 341, bemys bright 391, etc.

H : Rowes Rede 3, downe nor daale 9, notes nuwe 15, ful fayre and fressh 46, Bathed in bloode 136, reken or remembre 189, shoone so sheene 194, poynaunt as poysoun 201, Beten and bonched 206, sores for to sounde 268, trouble and tribulacioun 347, calle and crye 356, etc.

2. The Rhyme.

a. Quality of the Rhymes.

Most of the rhymes we find are pure, so that they would agree with Chaucer's system. Therefore I have taken this as the standard, and confine myself to pointing out only the differences. In both poems we find some peculiarities such as occur in Lydgate's works (Schick, *T. G.*, p. lx).

ǫ- and ǭ-rhymes (ten Brink, § 31; Bowen in *Englische Studien*, xx, p. 341):

In c: doñ 148 (p.p. O.E. ȝedôn), Anǫne 150 (O.E. onân).

In H: alsǫ 366 (O.E. ealswâ), hertǫ 368 (O.E. her-tô).

Doubtful is the rhyme: stoole 141 (N.E. *stole*), stoole 143 (N.E. *stool*). The first *stoole* is Lat. stŏla (στολή); O.E. stôle is, I suppose, not absolutely impossible (compare côc : cŏquum, scôl : scŏla, etc.), but modern English *stole* = sto^{u}l. Kluge in Paul's *Grundriss*, i. 931, has *stóle*, Sweet, *Student's Dictionary of Anglo-Saxon*, stole. The second stoole is surely O.E. stôl.

ę- and ę̄-rhymes:

In c: natiuitę 160, slę 161 (inf., O.E. slêan); Trinitę 289, thrę 291 (O.E. þrêo), Sęę 292 (O.E. sêe).

In H: fręę 328 (O.E. frêo), Sęę 329 (O.E. sêe).

In c, the rhyme here 111, 344 (inf., O.E. hêran)—were 112 (opt. pt., O.E. wêre) and—were 346 (pt. pl., O.E. wêron) is probably pure, as the Anglian form of *were* is *wêre*, *wêron*. In Chaucer it rhymes but in a few cases with ę, generally with ę̄ (ten Brink, § 25).

A good many *cheap rhymes* are found. Suffixes rhyming with each other, e. g. *in c:* -ence 2-4-5, 65-67-68, -ure 30-32-33; *in H:* -aunce 16-18-19, -acioun, -ouñ 198-200-201, -acle 317-319-320. Further e. g. *in c:* conceyue 134, deceyue 136; procede 155, succede 157; borñ 156, for-born 159; displese 230, plese 231; *in H:*

§ 4. *The Metre.*

dismembre 72, membre 74, Remembre 75; observe 107, conserve 109; heede 83, flesshlyhede 84. About the rhymes, *in c* hele 317 (subst.), hele 319 (verb), and *in H* stoole 141, stoole 143 compare ten Brink, § 330. Once, *in c,* we have the same word rhyming with itself: age ll. 298 and 299. Double forms occur of the verb *to die* :[1] The infinitive *deye* rhymes H 178 with *wey* 176 (dat. sg.) as well as c 107 the preterit singular *deyede* with *signifiede* 109 and *notified* 110. The same verb occurs in the rhyme e. g. c. ll. 75, 91, 166. eye (pl.) c. l. 100 rhymes with melodie 102 and sodenlye 103.

b. Number of rhyming syllables.

There can be no doubt that we have monosyllabic or strong rhymes *in c :* 29–31, 36–38, 43–45, etc.; *in H :* 20–21, 30–32–33, 55–56, etc., and dissyllabic or weak rhymes *in c :* 2–4–5, 6–7, 8–10, etc.; *in H :* 15–17, 16–18–19, 22–24, etc. Note the weak rhymes *in c :* séson 22, réson 24, and séson 58, réson 60, enchéson 61.[2] To the far greater number of lines we can rigorously apply Chaucer's standard for preserving the final -*e*, representing the different vowels of the old full endings. We shall find but a comparatively limited number of cases which will not agree with it.

There is first a very considerable number of -*i*, -*ie*-rhymes (ten Brink, § 327; Gattinger, p. 74 ff.). In the Temple of Glas—about 1403—no example of that kind of rhyme is found; in the Black Knight (1402–3) there are 3, in Horse, Goose, and Sheep (1436–40) none. (Compare *Deutsche Litteratur-Zeitung,* 1901, 33, p. 2074 ff.).

In c : ocy 90, dyë 91 (inf.).
    eyë 100 (pl.), melodië 102, sodenlye 103.
    crye 163 (O.Fr. cri), richly 165, dyë 166 (inf.).
    perfytly 282, multiplië 284 (inf.), viciously 285.
In H : sky 2 (O.N. ský), melody[ë] 4, Armonyë 5.
    melody[ë] 13, occy 14.

Other examples are as follows :—

In c : presencë 9, -tens 11 (O.Fr. temps), sentenscë 12.
    sense 16 (O.Fr. sens), eloquencë 18, sentencë 19.
    a-yeyn 226, paynë 228, restreynë 229 (inf.).
    lawe 254 (dat. sg.), to-drawë 256 (p.p.), sawe 257 (3. sg. pt.).
    a-wayte 302 (O.Fr. await), baytë 304 (O.N. beita).
    ys 331, myssë 333 (inf.), blisse 334 (dat. sg.).

---

[1] Schick, *T. G.*, p. lxi.
[2] Compare Skeat, *Chaucer,* vii. xiv. : géson 9, séson 11, tréson 12. *Ibid.* vii. vii. : réson 142, séson 144.

delitẹ 352 (O.Fr. delit), quitë 354 (inf.), appetitẹ 355 (O.Fr. appetit).

Doubtful: tendernessë 15, expressẹ 17.

diuinẹ 184 (O.Fr. divin), declynë 186 (inf.), matutyne 187. none 380 (dat. sg.), doñ 382 (p.p.), sonë 383 (O.E. sôna).

In H: messangier 44 (O.Fr. messager), chierë 46 (O.Fr. chiere), here 47.

apparailẹ 272 (O.Fr. appareil), raylë 273 (inf.).
tellë 295 (inf.), Danyell 297.
naturë 373 (O.Fr. nature), purẹ 375 (O.Fr. pur).

Doubtful: forsokë 160 (pl.), tookẹ 161 (sg.).

§ 5. THE LANGUAGE.[1]

A. DECLENSION.

I. *Substantives. Strong Masculines and Neuters.*

Nom. and Acc. without ending, but in H wey[ë] 350 (inorganic, see Schick, *T. G.*, p. lxv; Krausser, *Complaint*, p. 21; *Speculum Gy de Warewyke*, ed. by G. Morrill, p. clxix; *Pilgr.*, ll. 74. 4606).— *u-stem:* sonẹ 277.

Genitives in ës: in c: lordës 328, lyuës 408.—*Dissyllable* in ẹs: sómerẹs 36.

In H: sonës 24, briddës 51, 76, briddis 55, 59, 64.

Datives in ë: in c: slep[ë] 35.—2nd yere (?) 23.

In H: the following doubtful examples: daale 9, wey 176, morwe 344 (or mórow).—ja-stem: hewe 121.

In all other examples without ending.

Plural in ës:

In c: 1. *masc.:* bemës 93, bemys 391, othës 171, lordës 323; theves (?) 366, 375.—But angels 125.

2. *neutr.:* braynës 31, cloudës 94, thingës 124, 173, folkës 356; yeres (?) 247.—Besides we find: childrẹ 311 (elision) and two examples of the old plural without ending: thing 260 and folk 279.

In H: 1. *masc.:* fowlis 4, thevës 174, thornës 191, stonës 330.— i-stem: wittës 184.—*Dissyllables* in ẹs: lóvers 17, 63; besides: showrẹs 338 (rh. paràmours 340).

2. *neutr.:* grassis 39, folkës 266, sorës 268.—in ẹs: folkẹs 204. —in ën: childrën 328.

[1] On the principles followed in this paragraph, compare Schick, *T. G.*, p. lxiv and lxv, note 2.

§ 5. *The Language.*

One example of the old plural: folk 89.

Strong Feminines.

Nom. Neither of the poems has any example with sounded *e*, there are but disputable cases:
In *c*: goodnesse 8 (ten Brink, § 207, 2), queene 62.
In *H*: qwene 35, synne 70, sorwe 181 (or sórow).
Genitives: louës c. 14 and mankyndë H. 323.
Dat. and Acc. The ending is preserved:
In *c*: worldë 48.—In some cases it is doubtful whether the *e* was pronounced or not: lustynesse 10, tale 35, shame 56, swetnesse 89, ryght-wisnesse 204, wrechednesse 206, synne 212, snare 244, sake 266, youth 272, reuth 372, trewth 374,[1] mynde 378, tyde 389. But there are many examples where the *e* was evidently mute: loue 20, tyde 102, synne 118, helle 126, 144, byrth 169, sothfastnes 184, world 210, 278, soule 244, 315, 334, wonde 319, rode 364.

In *H*: lovë 29, 68, sakë 110, blissë 243, synnë 279; but downe 9, myght 31, love 35, 96, 109, hede 98, 368, worlde 349. Doubtful cases are love 43, honde 64, synne 70, reklesnes 90, kyndenesse 91, sake 97, mone 157, mekenesse 225, clennesse 227, wounde 270, boote 323, sorwe 346 (or sórow).

Plural in ës.

In *c*: handës 255, soulës 303, 396, tydës 341; myrthes (?) 74.

In *H*: Rowës 3, woundis 113, 287, synnës 183, 223, talës 202, handis 240, gyftës 245, kyndenessës 281; handis 114, 208. The old form of the Dat. Pl. is preserved in H 310 Whilom.

Weak Nouns.

1. *Masculines.*

Nom. wele c. 153 and bowe H 24 are doubtful; the e was certainly mute in: nek c. 255.

Genit. in ës: Crabbës H 1.

Dat. and Acc. No conclusive example of sounded ë, all the examples being dubious: *in c:* tyme 80, 197, 242, smert 223, wele 320; but tyme 382.

In H: mone (?) 48, tene (?) 193.

Plural. In c occurs but sterrës 283 and feres (?) 249; in H: sterris 38, dropës 150; but dropes 121.

---

[1] Compare Skeat, *Chaucer:* V. *Tr.* 1385-6, and I. *Book of the Duchesse,* 97-8.

xxviii § 5. *The Language.*

2. *Feminines.*

Nom. Again no conclusive example of sounded ë. *In c·*nyghtyngale 337, 393 are doubtful; but hertẹ 47 and sunnẹ 390.
In H: nyghtyngale (?) 355.—lady as vocative occurs 20, 24, 30.
Gen. in ës: hertis c. 62.
Dat. and Acc. In c: in ë: the single hertë 138; the others disputable: nyghtingale 34, throte 40, hert 128, 397 (enumeration), smert 223, hele 317, side 387. Certainly ẹ have hert 52, 270, 295, sydẹ 236.
In H: nyghtyngale 11, side 26, 114, 164, hert 95, smert 96, pride 233, almesse 241, all dubious; in ẹ, with certainty, erth 215.
Plural in ës: hertis c. 21 and sidës H 273, 305.

3. *Neuters.*

Plural: eye (?) c. 100.—Iën H 194.

Root-stems.

In H we find the two old plural forms: feetẹ 114, 210, 283 and men 209, 299. Besides there occur:
Gen.: in c: fadrës 183, but mannẹs 261.
In H: mannës 97, 110, 169, 193, 197, 230, 357, 365; faders 274.
Plural: in H: bookës 331; fiendẹs 317.
Gen.: in H: feendis 286, 294.
Note: crysten-man / Soule c. 115/6.

Romance Nouns.[1]

Singular: We have the French -e preserved: *in c:* peplë 285, tiercë 342; *in H:* spousë 360. Only in c occur (10) cases where the -*e* was certainly mute: gracẹ 154, voicẹ 178, vicẹ 215, Iugẹ 254, primẹ 268, croun 312, peynẹ 315, tiercẹ 337, syxtẹ 365, 378.

Polysyllables, with the accent thrown back, have -ẹ: *in c:* prýnses 1, Córagẹ 22, náturẹ 46, 75, ríchessẹ 164, etc. (ll. 180, 182, 213, 219, 257, 263, 265, 329, 354); also: mélodýẹ 104.—*in H:* náturẹ 6, séntencẹ 56, fóly 60, máner 70, cústom 107, súffrauncẹ 144, fýnauncẹ 147, málicẹ 288; also: mélodý 13.

Plural: in ës: in c: notës 66, 69, 83, 87, 338, peynës 314, 373, pryncës 323, agës 351, scornës 368.—*in H:* notës 15, 354, twnës 36, flourës 40, 118, peynës 210, clerkis 295.

Polysyllables have -ẹs, when the accent is thrown back: *in c:*

[1] In order to avoid a rather too big number of doubtful examples, I enumerate here only the unquestionable cases.

§ 5. *The Language.*

gálantųs 11, 267, bóffettęs 255, cítes 291, tórmentęs 367, but: discíplës 189.—*in H:* accúsours 139, vértuęs 142, but: Emeráwdës 34.

II. *Adjectives.*

ja- (*and i-*) *stems:* in *c:* grene (?) 63 (obl.)—*in H:* 1. *sg.:* triewë 69 (obl.); newe (?) 123 (acc.), swoote (?) 325 (acc.); deere (?) 360 (voc.); grene 359 (obl.) rhyming with: clene 361 (voc.). 2. *pl.:* grene (?) 34, kene (?) 191; nuwe 15 rhyming with: vntriewe 17.

The other adjectives have lost their inflexion in the singular. There are but two examples to be mentioned: *in c:* bare (?) 245 (acc.; see ten Brink, § 231; rhyming with: snare (?) 244 (obl.); comp. Skeat, *Chaucer*, II, *Tr.* I. 662).—*in H:* grete (?) 242 (acc.).

Plural: In c: derk[ë] 95; glade (?) 69, kynde (?) 377.

In H: white (?) 40, vnkynde (?) 106, 218, smale (?) 354.

In all the other cases ę.

The *weak form of the adjective* occurs:

1. *After the definite article.*

In c: Ded[ë] 292; but: myghty 3, gostly 16, lusty 58, gret 146, 234, holy 403.

In H: samë 11, sharp[ë] 61, gretë 67, 91(2), high[ë] 309, Redë 329, Right[ë] 350; white (?) 153 (pl.); but: bawmy 39, gretę 67, renomed 148, holy 221, clowdy 322.

2. *After a demonstrative pronoun.*

In c: this samë 73; but: this samę 223, This (That) hygh 148, 383, that (This) gret 208, 298.

No examples in H.

3. *After a possessive pronoun.*

In c: hyr ladyly 8, hyr high 9, his endles 122, thy (your) wor[l]dly 132, 153, Their filthi 288, theire besy 353.

In H: ourę gretë 99, his fairë 114, myn ownë 206, My fayrë 360; but: his holy 124, His blessyd 127, 249, 256, His hevenly 130, his holy 240, thyn old 342.

4. *Before proper names.*

In c: fresh[ë] May 25; but: All-myghty Ihesu 334, synfle Dathan 348.

In H: seynt Iohn 124, 164, 258, worthy Moyses 327, worthy David 331.

§ 5. The Language.

5. Before a vocative.
In c: welthy 152, synfull 190, 316, lusty 267, wrecched 316, myghty 323.
In H: vnkyndë creature 182, but: vnkynd 103, synful 337.

Romance Adjectives.

These generally keep their forms.

In c: strong: humblë 2, 181; stable 281 rhyming with: innvmerable 283; veray 24, curious 76, etc.—*weak:* noblë 6, proprë 55, tendrë 247; amerouse 12, troblus 48, etc.

In H: strong: noblë 318; purpure 121, perfite 238, etc.—*weak:* humblë 145; purpure 253, mortal 352, etc. The only exception is: his clierë H. 321 (ten Brink, § 242).

Plural: In c: fals[ë] 375; clere (?) 53; in all other cases we have the unchanged French forms: Desyrous 12, sure 326, etc.

In H: falsë 17; cliere (?) 36, 362, serpentyne (?) 315; the other forms are unchanged: fieblë 186; vicious 266, etc.—Weak forms in the plural do not occur.

III. Numerals.—Cardinals.

In c: one (*follows:* of) 167 (obl.); to 375, Bothe 114, 335, 349; thre 291; six 124; seuen 205; viii 209.

In H: oone 19 (obl. sg.), none 71, 125, etc. (acc. sg); two 81, tweyne (?) 174, 240 (comp. Schleich, *Fabula*, p. xlviii), both[ë] 81,[1] both 153, 344; fyvë 334 (before a noun), fyve (?) 184, 287, 330 (after a n.), fyve 118 (after a n.), 335 (before a n.), fyve 113, 115 (in the cæsura); seven 223; Fourty 231.

Ordinals: In c: first 121, 199 (follows: oure); 161 (adv.; in the cæsura); third 278, 299 (both followed by: age).—*In H:* first 120, 367 (adv.).

IV. Pronouns.

The same as in Chaucer. Therefore we mention only the following forms:

In c: hem 354 (C. theym), theym 15, 263, 305; theyr: in all cases; al: invariable in all cases; vch 143, 236.

In H: theym 20, them 26 (224 and 236 are taken from A), hym (= hem) 117, 282, hem: in all other cases (A has "them" throughout but l. 7 after: drought); theyr: in all cases; all: invariable, but alle (?) 183 (pl.; rhyming with: apalle 185); eche 187; thilk[ë] 97; —g. pl.: alre (??) 92.

[1] See also note to this line.

§ 5. *The Language.*

V. *Adverbs.*

In ë: in c: With-outë 31, 361; hyë (?) 72, 307, 324; expressë (?) 17; more (?) 209, a-twynne (?) 214. Surely: longe 81, sore 331, 333; when 92, 144, sone 148, 189, more 238, a-fore 242, 253.— *In H:* Withoutën 21, 27, 179, allonë 160, betwenë 174; blyve (?) 186, behynde (?) 220; surely: wrong 57.

In ës: in c: nedës 29, 157, (in, to) myddës 97, 99, 339, 340, 359, ellës 131, 322; but: nedes 181, elles 206.—*in H:* Towardës 2, oonës 213.

Besides numerous adverbs on -ly.

VI. *Composition.*

In c: primë-tens 23, day[ë]-rowes 54, slombrë-bed 57; kyndëly 33. *In H:* hert[ë]-bloode 112; kyndënesse 91, mekënesse 232; triew[ë]ly 56.

In the other examples we have: *in c:* prime-tens 11; godely 51, swetnesse 89, endles 122, 133, etc.; *in H:* sperhed 158; gretely 3; falsehede 28, mekenesse 225, etc.

B. CONJUGATION.

Infinitives. In both poems the number of examples with undoubtedly sounded ë is very small. We find *in c:* endurë 81, helë 223, thenkë 232, suffrë 261, 264, 266 (but: suffre 399), perceyvë 271; *in H:* wexën 120, 136, susteynë 131, suwën 163, makë 279, savë 306, rehersë 335, takën 337, Relevë 378.

Much larger is the number of forms with mute e, e. g.: *in c:* tabide 84, deseuer 167, dye 168, remord 190, thenke 192, folow 195, lye 222, etc. (26 examples); *in H:* herken 13, take 16, marke 26, wounde 26, se 49, pay 99, seen 127, etc. (29 examples). The dropping of *n* is proved by the rhyme in: dye c. 91 (rhyming with: ocy c. 90), sle c. 161 (rhyming with: natiuite c. 160), mysse c. 333 (rhyming with: ys c. 331); flee H 165 and tee H 166 (rhyming with: me H 163, se H 207, 237, 311, 367 (rhyming with French words ending in -ité and tre H. 208, 309).

We find, 15 times in c, 14 times in H, infinitives rhyming with each other; these, as well as about 35 doubtful cases in c, 31 in H, may still have been pronounced in Lydgate's time with ë, e. g.: *in c:* dresse 1, enbrace 13, apere 25, dye 75, expresse 88, here 111, etc.; *in H:* knowe 22, abyde 23, espye 28, avaunce 63, crye 105, vnclose 113, etc.

Indicative Present. 1. *sg.*: *in c:* gesse (?) 86.—*In H:* Reherse (?) 281; trowe (?) 15, calle (?) 363 (indecisive); certainly: cast 52.

§ 5. The Language.

2. *sg.: in c:* vsüst 171, entrëst 240; but: lyuest 172, standest (?) 191.—*In H:* Takestow (?) 71.

3. *sg.: in c:* Meuëth 34, sesëth 37, tellëth 114, owëth 116, endyth 199, hatëth 217, be-tokenëth 278, knokkëth 325; desireth 225 rhyming with: expyreth 227; but: loueth 46, cometh 159, perseuereth 275; contracted forms (ten Brink, § 186) in: set 35, a-byt 275 (rhyming with: yit 277 and hyt 278), probably in: biddeth = bit 166, perhaps also in: rewardeth 357, 361.—*In H:* Betokenyth 66, Syngëth 72, Streynëth 73, peynëth 73, meanyth 82, takith 83, cryëth 106; doubtful: meanyth 56, takith 65, Resownyth 84; but: Shakith 74, qwakyth 74, Callith 365, 366; contracted forms occur in: list 345, 348.

Plural: in c: be-seche 411.—*In H:* passën 176, darë 292; take (?) 98, pressen (?) 152, trespas (?) 204, specifie (?) 331; seen 292.

Subjunctive: in c: 2. *sg.*: lust 174, dye (?) 198; 3. *sg.:* Luste 9. —*In H:* 2. *sg.:* list 50, advert 77, ride (?) 117; 3. *sg.:* list 207, 237, 367, beholdë 311, see 311.

Imperative: in c: conceyue (?) 134, wep (?) 175; but certainly: Ryse 56, Enprinte 128, arme 129, Saue 131, let 138, 222, etc. (13 examples); *plural:* Entendëth 363; Beth 325; but: Let 268, Restreyne 270, Call 327, thenk 335.—*In H:* considrë 85, remembrë 225, gadrë 341; but in all other cases e: sle 20, bryng 21, Let 26, Cherissh 30, herkne 35, Rise 49, etc. (22 examples).—Of the *plural* occurs but the indecisive form: Lift 177.

Participle Present. With the exception of: langwisshyng (?) H 29 (pl.; rhyming with: bryng 31 (inf.)), we have but invariable forms in both poems.

Verbal noun, in -ing: in c: the norishing 30, the enduryng 40, my conny[n]ge 112, the begynny[n]g 121; mornyng 70, wepyng 163, connyng 177, etc.—*In H:* the meanyng 13, Thyn vndrestondyng 81, hir synggyng 83, myn heryng 185, The kepyng 258; meanyng 69, Smellyng 186, lokyng 197, heringe 202, towchyng 207, mysfotyng 209.

Strong Preterit. "Ablaut" as in Chaucer; so we mention but the following forms: *in c: sg.:* can = gan 136, 339, 395; leep 59, Fell 126; *pl.:* can = gan 54, ran 236, came 279, sank 290.—*In H: sg.:* can = gan 144; fille 42; *pl.:* drough 7, can = gan 19, saugh 125, d[r]ewe 171, Sawe 178, shoone 194; forsoke 160 rhyming with: tooke 161 (*sg.*).

Weak Preterit. In ëd, ed: in c: sg.: walkëd 61, romëd 64,

§ 5. *The Language.*

cesëd 88, expirëd 107, causëd 137, enterëd 161, suffrëd 257, 321, Openëd 349, Thirlëd 387, Ascendëd 402 ;. but : conceyued 68, manaced 161, swolowed 349. Doubtful are the following forms : rehersed 50, deyede 107, signifiede 109, suffred 193, 315, 371, reserued 205, cesed 233, ailed 367, died 371, expired 388.—*pl.*: offrëd 369 ; enchesoned 84, perysched 209, passed 300 ; presed (?) 236, desyred (?) 386.

In H : sg.: thrillëd 128, suffrëd 188, 199, 205, 242, trespassëd 211, offendid 213, shewëd 260, hastëd 261, venqwisshëd 336 ; but : priked 62, lyved 231. Doubtful is : suffred 270.—There occurs one single example of the 2. person : herdëst 58.—*pl.:* Receyvëd 314.

In dë, të, de, te.: in *c:* seide 60, sayd 73 ; made (?) 70, 179 ; thoght 91, lust 186, sent 403 ; a-lyght (?) 96 ; pl. indecisive : set 312. —*In H:* taught[ë] 6 ; herde 36, sayde 203, Spradde 235, made 325, 328 ; list 110, past 248, stynt 324 ; pl. left 171, 173.

Participle Past. Strong: in c: vnderstondën 120, etën 151, Takën 253, 298 ; but : ouerflow 212, slayn 400. Doubtful are : borñ 156, 313, for-born 159 rhyming with : be-forn 158, taken 188 rhyming with : for-saken 189, to-drawe 256 ; yeuen 397.—The sole plural form : bounde 255 is indecisive.

In H: stongën 95, foundë 141, Betën 206 ; doubtful are : borne 8, lorne 60, founde 271 ; Forsaken 170 and spoken 202 (pl.); plural besides in : founde 218, but undecisive.

Weak : in ëd : in c: declarëd 17, considrëd 19, renouelëd 23, entrëd 45, blessëd 50, formëd 123, etc. (27 cases).—*In H:* -huwëd 2, sugrëd 5, callïd 25, gouernëd 57, Rootëd 69, Steynëd 135, Blessyd 143, made = makëd 298, etc. (17 cases).

In ed (t): in c: Meued 22, herd 101, brent 133, past 239, 247, keept 248, etc. (10). Doubtful are the participles rhyming with each other as : exiled 27, reconciled 28, etc., or with preterits as : notified 110, etc.—*In H:* Spreynt 121, I-left 220 (compare : I-blent 130, Imeynt 137), Meynt 347. Rhyming are : to-Rent 127, spent 129, I-blent 130 ; depeynt 134, Imeynt 137, atteynt 138.

Polysyllables and contracted forms: in c: ráueshed 52, enlúmyned 95, púniched 237, fýnysched 274, bányshid 383 ; sprad 93, bent 255, put 263, hurt 318, fed 409.—*In H:* fúlfilled 197 ; Fret 34, sent 224, sprad 298.

About : infecte c. l. 143 see note to this line.

§ 6. THE AUTHORSHIP.

The first of our poems is cited by Tanner as 'Philomela' among Lydgate's works. In his *Bibliotheca Britannico-Hibernica* (1749), p. 491, l. 11 f. a., we read :

A saying of the nightingale signifying Christ: Ad Annam duciss. Buckingh. Pr. pr. prosa. "*It is seyd that the nightingale.*" *Pr. l.* "*Go lityll . . . prynces dresse.*" *MS. Cotton. Caligula A II. MS. C. C. C. Oxon. 203.*

Besides him, only Ritson mentions the title of our poems in his *Bibliographia Poetica* (1802), but, unfortunately, he has rather lost ground since the publication of Dr. Schick's *T. G.* (see p. cxlviii ff.).[1] In his long list of Lydgate's writings Ritson quotes as No. 213 :

A saying of the nightingale touching Christ: "*In Iune whan Titan was in Crabbes hede*" (*Caligula A. II. & the Harley MS. 2251*).

And indeed, we immediately meet with his incorrectness; for the title and the first line of the poem he cites agree only with H (or A; but this he apparently was not aware of). As to c, he seems to have known the MS. and the poem as one of Lydgate's works, but afterwards, when compiling his *Bibliographia*, the similar subject led him astray, and he forgot that neither the title nor the beginning of the poem was the same as in H (and A).

If we had no other argument than this statement of Ritson's to bring forward in favour of Lydgate's authorship, we could hardly venture to support our opinion. But Tanner's judgment is much more reliable, and, besides his authority, the internal evidence is, as we shall see, so striking, that we cannot but attribute this first poem to Lydgate. As the poem has not yet been printed, we need not wonder that the common sources like Bale and Pits do not mention it.

The second poem is acknowledged as one of the monk's works by Stowe : both MSS. got their titles from the hand of this chronicler, and at the end of A we find : *Of this Balade Dan Iohñ Lydgate made nomore.* This testimony of Stowe is the more valuable, as it goes back, according to his own words (see § 2), to Shirley. Then [1802] again we may refer to Ritson, and, at last, to *Warton-Hazlitt*, iii, 53, note 1 :

"*Lydgate in his Philomela, mentions the death of Henry Lord Warwick, who died in 1446. MS. Harl. ibid. (2251). 120. fol. 255.*"

Though this statement about Lord Warwick is disputed, as we

---

[1] But compare also: Brotanek, *Die Englischen Maskenspiele.* [*Wiener Beiträge zur Englischen Philologie xv.*] Wien, 1902, p. 9.

§ 6. *The Authorship.*

shall see (compare § 7), the notice nevertheless gives evidence that Warton and Hazlitt considered the H-version to be one of Lydgate's works.

Examining and comparing the style of the poems, which offers the strongest support in favour of Lydgate's supposed authorship, I venture to remark that it is superfluous to cite examples from H, as all said about c may also, *mutatis mutandis*, be applied to H.

Firstly, as we have seen, the metre in c is the same as in H. We have ǫ- and ǫ-rhymes, ę- and ę-rhymes (not, however, -ere and -ire- rhymes, as in the *T. G.*, p. lxi); the disregard of the final e in the rhymes has made progress; we find, e. g., a considerable number of i- and ie- rhymes. Other licences of Lydgate as to the structure of the verse exhibit themselves throughout the poem (see § 4; especially type C.), so that we are fully authorized in claiming the evidence of the metre in support of Lydgate's authorship. The language, in the main, shows the same character as, for instance, the language of the Temple of Glas, Complaint of the Black Knight, and Horse, Goose and Sheep; compare the outlines of grammar in the editions of Dr. Schick, Dr. Krausser, and Dr. Degenhart.

Again, the style is entirely Lydgatian. As we have no convincing external evidence, we may be allowed to draw the special attention of the reader to the peculiarities of Lydgate, found in the first poem. When we compare Dr. Schick's remarks about the monk's style (*T. G.*, p. lxxxiv and cxxxiv ff.; see also Gattinger, p. 70 ff.), we must say, that—so far as the different subject does not exclude comparison—all these characteristics are to be observed in our poem. The very beginning of the poem gives us an argument:

"Go, lityll quayere, ..."—these introductory lines are entirely in accordance with his usage. Not only are the ideas, the expressions used in that stanza nearly all found in his envoys, so e. g.: *M. P.* 45, 48, 149; *Kk. I.*, f. 196 a; *T. G.*, ll. 1393[1]–1403, but even the characteristic "lityll" is not wanting, which he never forgets, be it a poem of 35 or 35,000 lines (*Falls*, 219 b 1). Though his favourite request "to correct" his poem[2] has not found a place in this very first stanza, he afterwards cannot conceal his self-depreciatory manner; compare ll. 18, 88/9, 112, 177, 181, 182.

Further, the astronomical allusions, ll. 25, 26, 45, 92, the framework of a vision, st. 7–15, the sleepy poet, l. 44, the season-motive, st. 4, the reference to his real or supposed source, ll. 108, 114, 238,

---

[1] See note to this line. [2] See note to l. 1400 of the *Temple of Glas*.

344, the use of Latin and foreign words, ll. 308, 388 (see Köppel, *Laurent's de Premierfait und Iohn Lydgate's Bearbeitungen von Boccaccio's De Casibus Virorum Illustrium*. München, 1885, p. 40), all these points are quite as common in Lydgate's works as are the numerous anacolutha which occur in this short poem; compare st. 4, 8, 9, 10, 13, 16, 20, 27, 34, and ll. 412, 413.

A pretty large number of Lydgatian stock phrases could be gathered from our poem; but on this point I had better refer the reader to Gattinger, pp. 72, 73 and Schleich, *Fabula*, p. 64 ff.

In respect to the theological matters, for instance, Pride the chief sin, etc., see Triggs, *Assembly*, Literary Studies, 10, 11, and the notes to our two poems.

All these points, I think, give evidence that the style of our poem is entirely in accordance with the common features of Lydgate's works. Besides, I shall give in the notes quotations from other poems of our poet, which will show that the whole atmosphere of the poem, the whole range of ideas, the vocabulary,[1] the motives and allegories are essentially the same as in the other works of the monk.

§ 7. THE DATE.

The first stanza of the c-version contains the dedication to a Duchess of Buckingham, which allows us to fix the date of the first poem pretty exactly.

> Go, lityll quayere, And swyft thy prynses dresse,
> Offringe thyselfe wyth humble reuerence
> Vn-to the ryght hyghe and myghty pryncesse,
> The Duches of Bokyngham, and of hur excellence
> Besechinge hyre, that, of hure pacyence,
> Sche wold the take, of hure noble grace,
> Amonge hyre bokys for the Asygne A place.

As the compiler of the index of MS. C rightly points out, this Duchess is Anne, daughter of Ralph Nevill, first Earl of Westmorland. Her mother was the Earl's second wife,[2] Ioan Beaufort, daughter of Iohn of Gaunt and his second wife, Katherine Roet, sister-in-law (?) to Chaucer.[3] She married Humphrey Stafford, who was created Duke of Buckingham 14 September, 1444 (*D. N. B.*

---

[1] e. g. adolescens c l. 267.
[2] He *m.* secondly, before 3 Feb. 1397, Joan (formerly Joan Beaufort, spinster), widow of Sir Robert Ferrers, the legitimated dau. of John (Plantagenet, called "of Gaunt"), Duke of Lancaster, by Catharine, da. of Sir Payne Roet.—G. E. C. *Complete Peerage*, viii. 111.
[3] See Skeat, *Chaucer* II, p. lxix, and I, p. li, § 43.

§ 7. *The Date.*

liii, p. 451).[1] This date fixes the *terminus a quo* to the last months of the year 1444.

We are fortunate enough to find another allusion in our poem which allows us to determine the date more closely: st. 48, ll. 330–333 we find:

> A myghty prince, lusty, yonge, & fiers,
> Amonge the peple sore lamented ys:
> The duc of Warwyk; entryng the oure of tierce
> Deth toke hym to whom mony sore shall mysse.

The Duke of Warwick who is mentioned in these lines, is Henry Beauchamp, Duke of Warwick (from April 5, 1444), and is said (without evidence) to have been King of Wight, Jersey and Guernsey[2] from 1445. The date of his death is disputed. It is given as June 11, 1445, by *D. N. B.*, iv, p. 28 *b* and the *Nouvelle Biographie Générale*, p. 556; but neither of these, nor both combined, can stand against the best authority, Mr. G. E. Cokayne, who in his *Complete Peerage*, viii. 59 (1898), adopts the date given by Baker in his *Northamptonshire* ii. 219, 11 June (1446), 24 Hen. VI. This is confirmed by the grant of Letters of Administration to him on 17 June 1447 at Lambeth. He was the son of Richard Beauchamp, Earl of Warwick, d. at Rouen, 4 Oct. 1439, regent of France during the absence of the Duke of Bedford (*D. N. B.* iv, p. 29 a–31 a),[3] and brother-in-law to Richard Nevill, who married Anne, Henry's sister and heiress,[4] in whose right he was created afterwards Earl of Warwick, and who is well-known as the

---

[1] In the *Nouvelle Biographie Générale*, vii, p. 707, however, we find the notice: En 1445, ce comté [Buckingham] passa à la maison de Stafford, dans la personne d'Edmond, comte de Stafford, qui fut fait Duc de Buckingham l'année suivante.

[2] "He is asserted (*Mon. Ang.* ii. 63; Leland's *Itinerary*) to have been, also, crowned *King of the Isle of Wight*, by Henry [VI], but for this (Coke, *4th Inst.*, p. 287; Stubbs's *Const. Hist.* iii. 433) there is no evidence" (*Nat. Biogr.*, in an article written by J. H. Round).... He died without male issue at his birthplace, Hanley Castle, 11 June, 1446.—G. E. C. viii. 59.

[3] See also Schick, *T. G.*, p. xciii.

[4] One of the sisters. Earl Richard left 4 daughters, coheirs on the death of Duke Henry's girl Anne, b. at Cardiff in Wales, Feb. 1442-3, d. an infant, at Ewelme, Oxon. 8 Jan. 1448-9, and was bur. at Reading Abbey. "Those four coheirs, all of whom left issue, were (1) Margaret, m. John (Talbot), Earl of Shrewsbury, which Lady was mentioned in the entail of the Earldom of Warwick, cr. in 1450; (2) Eleanor, m. firstly Thomas (de Ros), Lord Ros, who d. 18 Aug. 1431, secondly Edmund (Beaufort), Duke of Somerset, slain 22 May 1455, and thirdly, Walter Rodesley; (3) Elizabeth, m. George (Nevill), Lord Latimer, who d. 30 Dec. 1469; (4) Anne, only da. by the second wife [Isabel, Baroness Burghersh, a grand-daughter of Edw. III.], who m. Richard (Nevill), Earl of Warwick, so cr. in 1449."—G. E. C. viii. 60. Duke Henry was 'scarce ten years of age' when he married in 1434. His father's first wife was seven years old when he wedded her.

"King-maker." This Richard was the nephew of the above-mentioned Anne, Duchess of Buckingham, to whom Lydgate dedicated the poem.

These facts confirm to a certain extent the authorship of Lydgate. As we find in Schick, *T. G.*, p. xciii, the poet was, during his sojourn in France, in the service of Lord Richard of Warwick, the father of Henry, mentioned in st. 48. Therefore we are not astonished to find this allusion in a poem of Lydgate's, the more so as the Duchess of Buckingham herself, to whom the poem is dedicated, was, as we have seen, the aunt of Henry's brother-in-law.

We must therefore fix the date of the c-version in the second half of the year 1446, considering that the poet says, "lamented ys," and that it is most probable that Lydgate's dedication to the Duchess Anne, she being related to the deceased Duke of Warwick, was in some way connected with this sad event.

As to the date of the other version it is no easy matter when we attempt to fix it. There are no allusions to historical events to be found in the poem. Only, the note by Stowe, at the end of H : Of this Balade Dan Iohn Lydgate made nomore,[1] might possibly induce us to date it before c, but a glance at the metre makes us immediately withdraw this conjecture, as the numerous examples of type D, for instance, would rather prove a later date. The language cannot help us, nor any other internal evidence, so that the best we can do, is to omit the fixing of any date at present; perhaps, later on, we may be more fortunate, and light upon some clue.

§ 8. THE SOURCES.

As we have already stated in a preceding paragraph, both poems have a common source, which is also referred to by the poet himself in MS. c, l. 108 :

> 106. This brid, of whom y haue to you rehersed,
> Whych in her song expired thus ande deyede,
> 108. In latyn fonde y in a boke well versed,

There are two "Latin Books" known under the title "Philomela." The one, of a fairly large size, is a work of John of

---

[1] As this statement was no doubt copied by Stow from his Shirley original, we may fairly compare it with the like entry in the Lydgate and Burgh's *Secree of Secrees* (?1446, Schick), after the poet's decease, and conclude that the cause of the break-off in the Nightingale poem was Lydgate's death. This is borne out by the character of the metre, as the many examples of type D tend to prove a late date.—F.

§ 8. The Sources.   xxxix

Hoveden (Howden, Yorkshire), but has nothing in common with our poems here but the title (compare *D. N. B.* xxvii, 427 *a* ff. and Hahn, Arnold, *Quellenuntersuchungen zu Richard Rolle's Englischen Schriften*. Halle, 1900, p. 3 and note). The other, the source of Lydgate's poems, is a shorter Latin poem, also called "Philomela," printed among Bonaventura's works, e. g. in the edition of Ad Claras Aquas (Quaracchi) 1882–1898, tom. viii, p. 669–674. This poem, the authorship of which is uncertain, was of great popularity during the Middle-Ages. At that time it was generally ascribed to Bonaventura,[1] but the editors of the edition above-mentioned reject his authorship,[2] whereas the probability of John Peckham[3] being the author is more likely. There are more than thirty Latin MSS.[4] extant, and many imitations and translations.[5] The poems here printed represent the English imitations; compare *Warton-Hazlitt*, i, p. 172 note; *D. N. B.* xxvii, p. 427; Schick, *T. G.*, p. xcvi and Addenda.

The two poems do not bear a like amount of resemblance to their model. MS. c follows much more closely than H (see later) the Latin poem, as a short analysis of the two will show.

Before we sketch the contents of the poems, we have a few remarks to make on the opening words in MS. C. In most of the MSS. of the Latin version we find prefixed to the poem a short admonitory treatise in prose, the genuineness of which is rejected by the editors of Bonaventura's works. Similarly, there is, in MS. C

---

[1] Lydgate, of course, was acquainted, at least in his way, with the works of Bonaventura; he cites him, e. g. *Court of Sapience*, e 6 *a* (? englisht his *Life of our Lady*).

[2] See S. Bonaventura opera omnia. Ad Claras Aquas (Quaracchi) 1898. 2º. tom. viii, p. 669, note 3, and Prolegomena c. III, a. 1, § 7.

[3] See *D. N. B.* xliv, p. 190 ff. (*Philomela*, p. 196 *a*) and Hook, W. F., *Lives of the Archbishops of Canterbury*. London, 1865. 4º. See also the article "Hoveden" in *D. N. B.* xxvii, p. 427, and Horstmann, *Yorkshire Writers*, ii, p. xxxix.

[4] Most of the MSS. are enumerated in the Prolegomena of the Quaracchi-edition, tom. viii. I only add the following: Pembroke College, Cambridge, B. 3. 19, Harl. 3766, Cotton Cleopatra A XII, Laud 402, Rawlinson C. 397 (Rawlinson C. 348 is but one leaf, missing in Rawlinson C. 397), Digby 28, University Library, Cambridge, Ee VI, 6.

[5] Philomena S. Bon. castellane traducta et dilatata carmine et prosa per cantus ipsius Philomenæ, by Mathaeus a Nativitate. Salmanticae, 1471.— Filomena de S. Bonaventura, sive tractatulus hoc titulo, Hispanice versus, by Ludovicus Granatensis. Adiciones al Memorial de la vida Christiana. Salmanticae, 1577.—S. Bonaventurae Philomena, editio carmine Italico, by Jacobus de Porta. Venetiis, 1586.—Die Nachtigall des hl. Bonaventura, by E. Vötter. München, 1612.—Melch. v. Diepenbrock, Geistlicher Blumenstrauss. Sulzbach, 1862 (pp. 302-333, with the Latin text).—The anonymous translation: Des hl. Bonaventura Philomele oder Nachtigallenlied. Lingen, 1883—and that by Leberecht Drewes were not accessible to me.

§ 8. *The Sources.*

only, a kind of prose introduction, not intended to suggest to the reader the necessary elevation of mind, but simply to give a concise epitome of the principal contents. These lines in C, however, reproduce the ideas of the poem so incorrectly that we cannot consider them as originally written by the poet, but must presume them to be the work of a scribe :

    Matutina—Beginning of the World, Fall of Adam, Nativity of Man, " patris sapiencia."
    Hora I.—Noah.
    [Hora III. =] " crucifige "—Abraham.
    Hora VI. ⎫ —Resurrection, Ascension, Pentecost, Corpus-Christi-
    Hora IX. ⎭   Day.

Compared with the real structure of the c-version below, this short analysis exhibits too serious discrepancies to allow us to attribute this introduction to Lydgate.

We now return to the comparison of the two poems :

Structure of the Latin Poem.

  St.   1-4 : Introduction,
        5-10 : The story of the nightingale,
      11-13 : General interpretation of the story and
      14-16 : of the single hours.

Then follow the special meditations of the different hours :

      17-24 : Matutina,
      25-34 : Prima,
      35-47 : Tertia,
      48-77 : Sexta,
      78-90 : Nona.

Structure of the c-version.

  St.   1-6 : Dedication and introduction,
      7-15 : The story of the nightingale,
        16 : The source,
        17 : General interpretation.

Then the meditations of the single hours follow :

      18-28 : Aurora,
      29-39 : Prime,
      40-48 : Tierce,
      49-54 : Sexte,
      55-59 : Nones.

§ 8. *The Sources.*

This shows clearly that the structure of the c-version is wholly borrowed from the Latin source. Lydgate only omitted the short interpretation of the hours, st. 14–16 of the Latin poem, to which we do not find corresponding lines in the c-version. But we must state that, though the story of the nightingale and the general interpretation are the same in both, the English poet treats different subjects in the meditations for the single hours. In the Latin source we have the following themes:

14. *Mane* vel *diluculum* hominis est status,
    In quo mirabiliter Adam est creatus.
    Hora prima, quando est Christus incarnatus,
    Tertiam die spatium sui incolatus.

15. *Sextam*, cum a perfidis voluit ligari,
    Trahi, caedi, conspui, dire cruciari,
    Crucifigi denique, clavis terebrari
    Caputque sanctissimum spinis coronari.

16. *Nonam* die, cum moritur, quando consummatus
    Cursus est certaminis, quando superatus
    Est omnino zabulus et hinc conturbatus.
    Vespera, cum Christus est sepulturae datus.

In the c-version we always find two subjects for each hour, one from the Old and the other from the New Testament, *i. e.* from the passion of our Lord:

Aurora: Creation of the world, fall of Lucifer, fall of Adam—Jesus taken Prisoner,
Prime: Noe—Christ before Pilate,
Tierce: Abraham, Sodom—Christ led to Calvary,
Sexte: Dathan and Abiron—Christ on the cross,
Nones: Adam banished—Christ dies.

This comparison proves that, though Lydgate adopted the general idea and the structure of the poem from Peckham, he was by no means a slavish imitator, but on the contrary followed his own bent.

Again we find another trace of Lydgate's originality. To the parallelism of the quotations from the Old and New Testament, he adds the comparison of the ages of man with the different hours of the daily divine service. At each hour he subsequently addresses people of another, higher age; compare

st. 23: "Aurora"—l. 156:
    Be-thenke thy-self, hough porely þu was borñ

§ 8. *The Sources.*

st. 35/6 : "Prime"—l. 239 :
    O thow, that hast thus past the oure of morow
l. 247 : Ande of thy tendre age art past the yeres,
st. 43/6 : "Tierce"—ll. 299, 300 :
    And namely ye that are in the third age
    Of your lyfe ande passed morow & prime,
ll. 316, 317 : Thenk on this oure, thou wrecched synfull man,
    That in this age hast reson, strenght, and hele,
st. 52 : "Sexte"—ll. 358, 359 :
    And, in speciall, ye of perfyt age,
    This oure of sixt, in myddes of your lyfe,
st. 59 : "Nones"—l. 412 :
    That, fro this worlde when so we shall deseuer.

I think we cannot carry the comparison further, as most of the ideas found in c are commonplaces, which do not rise above the average education of a priest in those times. Therefore, even when we find the same ideas in both poems, it is no proof that Lydgate borrowed them from Peckham.

The "Monk of Bury" had, of course, an extensive knowledge of Holy Scripture.[1] We give here a list of all lines to which parallel passages are to be found in the Bible, which I consider as Lydgate's second principal source. The references are from the Vulgate.

[114 : see note to this line].
ll. 121–124 : Gen. i.
ll. 125–126 : Is. xiv. 12–16.
[129, 130 : see note to these lines].
l. 133 : Mat. xxv. 41.
l. 136 : Gen. iii. 1–6.
ll. 139, 143 : Rom. v. 12.
ll. 150, 383 : Gen. iii. 23, 24.
[ll. 164–168 : see note to these lines].
l. 185 : Jo. i. 29.
l. 188 : Mat. xxvi. 48–50 = Mar. xiv. 44–46 = Lu. xxii. 47, 48, 54 = Jo. xviii. 5, 12.
l. 189 : Mat. xxvi. 56 = Mar. xiv. 50–52.
l. 203 : Gen. vii. 10.
l. 205 : Gen. vii. 13.
ll. 206–208 : Gen. vii. 21.

---

[1] See Köppel, l. c., p. 48 f., Gattinger, p. 37/8, and again Koeppel in *Englische Studien* 24 (1898), p. 281 f.

§ 8. *The Sources.* xliii

l. 220 : 1 Pet. i. 18, 19.
l. 224 : Lu. xv. 7, 10.
ll. 225–226 : Ezech. xxxiii. 11; (Sap. i. 13); 2 Pet. iii. 9.
ll. 235, 279–280 : Gen. x.
ll. 236 : Gen. xi. 1–9, xiii. 13, xviii. 20, 21.
l. 244 : 2 Tim. ii. 26.
l. 252 : Mat. xxvi. 59–60 = Mar. xiv. 55–59.
ll. 253–254 : Mat. xxvii. 2, 11 = Mar. xv. 1 = Lu. xxiii. 1 = Jo. xviii. 12, 28, 29.
ll. 257–259 : Mat. xxvi. 67 (xxvii. 30) = Mar. xiv. 65 (xv. 19).
l. 260 : 2 Macc. vii. 28 = Hebr. xi. 3.
ll. 262–263 : Mat. xxvi. 53.
ll. 271–272 : Prov. v. 6.
ll. 281–282 : Gen. xv. 6.
ll. 283–284 : Gen. xv. 5.
ll. 291 : Gen. xix. 24, 25.
l. 296 : Gen. i. 27.
ll. 302–303 : 1 Pet. v. 8.
ll. 307–308 : Mat. xxvii. 23 = Mar. xv. 13, 14 = Lu. xxiii. 21 = Jo. xix. 6, 15.
l. 310 : Mat. xxvii. 28 = Mar. xv. 17 = Jo. xix. 2, 5.
l. 311 : Jo. xix. 4, 5.
l. 312 : Mat. xxvii. 29 = Mar. xv. 17 = Jo. xix. 2, 5.
l. 313 : Jo. xix. 17.
l. 314 : Mat. xxvii. 33 = Mar. xv. 22 = Lu. xxiii. 33 = Jo. xix. 17.
ll. 348–350 : Num. xvi. (1, 2) 31–33.
l. 365 : Mat. xxvii. 31 (45) = Lu. xxiii. 33 (44) = Jo. xix. 18, but Mar. xv. 24, 25 (see ll. 379, 380).
ll. 366, 375 : Mat. xxvii. 38 = Mar. xv. 27 = Lu. xxiii. 33 = Jo. xix. 18.
ll. 367–368 : Mat. xxvii. 48 (34) = Mar. xv. 36 (23) = Lu. xxiii. 36 = Jo. xix. 29, 30.
l. 384 : Gen. iii. 17–19.
ll. 385, 387 : Jo. xix. 34.
l. 386 : Jo. xix. 31.
ll. 388–389 : Mat. xxvii. 46, 50 = Jo. xix. 30 (Mar. xv. 34, 37, Lu. xxiii. 46).
ll. 390–392 : Mat. xxvii. 45 = Mar. xv. 33 = Lu. xxiii. 44, 45.
l. 399 : Mat. xxvi. 28 = Mar. xiv. 24 = Lu. xxii. 20.

ll. 401–402 : Mat. xxviii. 1–10 = Mar. xvi. 1–8, 19 = Lu. xxiv. 1–12, 51 = Jo. xx. 1–10 = Act. i. 9, 10.
l. 403 : Act. ii. 1–4.
ll. 404–406 : Mat. xxvi. 26 = Mar. xiv. 22 = Lu. xxii. 19.

This detailed list of references will, I hope, justify my opinion as to Lydgate's being influenced by the Bible.

The two sources which I have just investigated with regard to the first poem, have also exercised their influence on the H-version, though here the imitation of Peckham's work is by no means a close one. We may sketch the structure of the second poem as follows:

st. 1–5 : Introduction : Secular interpretation of the song of the nightingale,
st. 6–7 : The vision, in which the poet is addressed by an angel from heaven,
st. 8–15 : Beginning of the heavenly messenger's tale, he introducing the nightingale meditating on Christ's passion.
st. 16–22 : Her song, in which are contained :
st. 23–33 : The words which Christ speaks.
st. 34–54 : The nightingale's song goes on, but is not finished.

Were the poem complete, we should expect to find the end of the nightingale's song, the end of the angel's speech, and the conclusion of the vision. It seems that the poet found the task too tiresome, or he had some other reasons; at all events, he did not finish his work—no doubt he died. We see, however, that here the structure of the Latin original is totally abandoned, the different hours are not even mentioned; only the general idea of a religious interpretation of the nightingale's song is retained.

As to the other principal source, the Bible, the following list will show to what extent the poet has put his theological knowledge into this poem :

ll. 95, 158, 212 : Jo. xix. 34.
l. 101 : see c, l. 365.
ll. 111–112 : see c, l. 399.
ll. 122–123 : Mat. xxvii. 59 = Mar. xv. 46.
ll. 124, 162, 164, 257, 258 : Jo. xix. 25–27.
ll. 128, 191 : see c, l. 312.
ll. 134, 135, 141, 142 : Is. lxiii. 1.
ll. 137, 196, 201, 265 : see c, l. 368.
l. 138 : see c, l. 254.

§ 8. *The Sources.*

l. 139 : see c, l. 252.
ll. 148–156, 167–168, 304 : Is. lxiii. 2–3.
l. 157 : Mat. xxvii. 50 = Mar. xv. 37 = Lu. xxiii. 46.
ll. 160, 165, 170, 173 : see c, l. 189.
l. 174 : see c, l. 366.
ll. 179, 211, 213 : 2 Cor. v. 21 = 1 Pet. ii. 22.
l. 206 : Mat. xxvi. 67, xxvii. 30 = Mar. xiv. 65, xv. 19 = Lu. xxii. 63, 64 = Jo. xviii. 22, xix. 3.
l. 226 : Lu. ix. 58 (ii. 7).
l. 231 : Mat. iv. 2 = Mar. i. 13 = Lu. iv. 1, 2.
l. 232 : Jo. xix. 30.
ll. 246–248 : see c, l. 404.
l. 249 : Mat. xxvi. 27, 28 = Mar. xiv. 23, 24 = Lu. xxii. 20.
l. 252 : Jo. xix. 34.
ll. 253–254 : Jo. xix. 23, 24 (Mat. xxvii. 35, Mar. xv. 24, Lu. xxiii. 34).
ll. 255–256 : Mat. xxvii. 57–61 = Mar. xv. 42–47 = Lu. xxiii. 50–56 = Jo. xix. 38–42.
l. 259 : Lu. xxiii. 46.
l. 264 : Jo. xviii. 19, 22, 23.
ll. 276–280 : Jo. iii. 16, 17.
ll. 289–290 : see c, ll. 313, 314.
ll. 297–298 : Dan. iv. 7–9, 17–19.
ll. 300–301 : Gen. xxxii. 10.
l. 302 : Gen. xxviii. 12.
l. 303 : Job xl. 20.
ll. 307–308 : 1 Reg. xvi. 23.
st. 45 : Num. xxi. 8–9.
ll. 318–319 : Ezech. ix. 4–6.
l. 320 : Ex. xxxvii. 17.
l. 325 : Ex. xv. 23–25.
ll. 327–329 : Ex. xiv. 16, 21, 22.
ll. 330–333 : 1 Reg. xvii. 40, 49, 4.
ll. 353–354 : Cant. iv. 8, etc.
l. 358 : Cant. v. 1.
l. 374 : Jo. i. 14.
l. 375 : Lu. i. 28.
l. 377 : Is. xi. 1, 10.

This list, even somewhat longer than the first, likewise shows Lydgate's knowledge of the Scriptures.

xlvi   § 9. *Concluding Remarks.*

I first intended to collect all the lines which show the influence of other works, and give them here, but I preferred putting this material into the notes, in order to avoid repetition, as many of these quotations at the same time serve to illustrate Lydgate's language and style. I draw the attention of the reader to the notes to c, l. 90 and H, l. 5.

§ 9. CONCLUDING REMARKS.

I insert this last paragraph for the sole reason of giving a short summary of the researches.[1]

Lydgate's *Nightingale* exists in two versions: one dates from the second half of the year 1446, the other is of uncertain date[2] and unfinished. Two MSS. of each version are preserved, and the texts are, on the whole, carefully handed down. Metre, language, and style are in accordance with Lydgate's general usage. As principal sources of the two poems, we find John Peckham's Latin poem " Philomela" and the Bible.

[1] Compare Schick, *T. G.*, p. xcv and xcvi.   [2] See p. xxxviii, note 1.

I.

The Nightingale.

[PROSE. INTRODUCTION. Not by Lydgate:
see p. xl.]

[MS. C.C.C.O. 203, p. 1] *Assit principio sancta Maria
meo. Amen.*

¹ it is seyd that the nyghtyngale of hure nature *The night-*
hathe A knowleche of hure deth. And, lyke as *ingale,*
the swañ syngeth Afore his deth, so sche, in the day *before her*
of hure deth, Assendyth in-to the top of the tre and *death, flies to a*
v syngeth In hora matutina A lame[n]table note; and *tree-top, and there,*
so aftyre, by mene degrees Aualynge lowere, hora *at the hours of divine*
prima, hora tercia, hora sexta, et hora nona, tyll sche *service (Prime, Tierce, Sexte,*
com doun in-to the myddys of the tre. And there, in *and Nones), sings mourn-*
hora nona, sche dyeth. This ys moralysyd vn-to *ful notes, till in the*
x Cryste An[d] in-to euery crystyñ sowle, that schuld *tree-midst she dies.*
remembre the ourys of Cristys passyoun. And allso *These songs are meant to*
by 'hora matutina' ys vndurstondeñ the begynnynge *be a commemoration*
of the world, and the gret fall of owre ffadure Adam, *of Christ's passion.*
and the natyuite of euery mañ, And 'patris sapiencia'
xv declared; and in like wyse 'hora prima, Crucifige,
hora sexta, And hora nona' declared wyth the Ages
of the worlde in tyme of Noe and of Abraham, And
so forthe brefly touched the Resurectioun, the Ascencyone, pentecost, And Corpus Cristi day et cetera.

---

¹ *For the wanting capital, see description of* C.   vii. prima]
a *above the line.*   tercia] *see note to this line.*   viii. of] *follows* o.
ix. moralysyd] ysy *illegible.*   xiii. Adam] a *above the line.*
xiv. patris] *the first half illegible.*   xvii. Abraham] a *above the line.*

I. *The Proem and Dedication.*

[PROEM. THE DEDICATION.]

[59 *stanzas of sevens, ababbcc.*]

(1)

<small>Go, little poem, present thyself to the</small>

Go, lityll quayere, And swyft thy prynses dresse, 1
  Offringe thyselfe wyth humble reuerence
Vn-to the ryght hyghe and myghty pryncesse,

<small>Duchess of Buckingham, and ask her for a place [p. 2] among her books,</small>

  The Duches of Bokyngham, and of hur excellence
    Beseechinge hyre, that, of hure pacyence 5
  Sche wold the take, of hure noble grace
  Amonge hyre bokys for the Asygne A place, 7

(2)

<small>till she reads thee to her courtiers,</small>

Vn-to the tyme hyr ladyly goodnesse 8
  Luste for to call vn-to hyr high presence
Suche of hyre peple, that are in lustynesse
  Fresschly encoragyt, as galant*us* in p*r*ime-tens,
    Desyrous for to here the amerouse sentensce 12
  Of the nyghtyngale, and in there mynde enbrace,
  Who fauoure moste schall fynd in loues g*r*ace, 14

[MS. Cott. Calig. A ii, leaf 59.]

(3)

Commandyng theym to here wyth tendernesse 15

<small>to show them how to interpret the nightingale's song truly, *i. e.* in a spiritual sense.</small>

  Of this your nightyngale the gostly sense,
Whos songe and deth declared is expresse
  In englysh here, right bare of eloquence,
    But notheles considred *the sentence : 19
  All loue vnlawfle, y hope, hit will deface
  And fleschly lust out of theyre hertis chace, 21

(4)

Meued of Corage be vertu of the seson, 22
  In p*r*ime-tens renoueled yere be yere,
Gladyng eu*er*y hert of veray reson,

<small>The fresh season of May banishes the cold of winter.</small>

  When fresh[e] May in kalendes gan apere,
    Phebus ascendyng, clere schynyng in hys spere, 26
  By whom the colde of wyntyr is exiled
  And lusty seson thus newly reconciled. 28

<small>1 lityll—And] *illegible by dirt.*   2 Offringe thyselfe] *illegible by dirt.*   4 Bokyngham] a *above the line.*   19 the] de c.   21 out] *above the line* c.   24 veray] a *preceding* verray *blotted out* c.</small>

I. *In May the Nightingale bids me rise.*

(5)

To speke of sleep, hit nedes most be had 29 *All creatures want sleep during the night;*
  Vnto the norishing of euery creature,—
With-oute whech braynes must be mad,
Outragesly wakyng oute of mesure,—
Excepte thoo that kyndely nature 33 *the nightingale alone can spend this time watching.*
  Meueth to wach, as the nyghtingale,
Whych in her seson be slep[e] set no tale. 35

(6)

For sche, of kynde, all the someres nyght 36 *She sings all night.*
  Ne seseth not with mony a lusty note,
Wheder hit be dry or wete, derk or lyght,
Redly rehersyng her leson ay be rote—
Gret mervell is the enduryng of hir throte— 40
  That her to here it is a second heuen,
So melodiouse ande mery is her steuen. 42

[THE POEM.]

(7)

And, on a nyght in Aprile, as y lay 43 *Near the end of April, I was lying sleepless,*
  Wery of sleep & of my bed all-so,
Whene that the kalendes entred were of May
(Whech of hir nature neither loueth of thoo),
My herte with mony a thoght was ouer-go 47 *troubled with heavy thoughts.*
  Ande with this troblus worlde sore agreued,
But, as god wold, in hast y was Releued. 49

(8)

Thys blessed brid, of whom y you rehersed, 50 [leaf 59, bk.]
  As fer as that y godely myght hir here,
So thorghly my hert raueshed had and persed   *Long before day-break, I fancied that the nightingale by her ravishing song summoned me to follow her.*
  Ryght with hir longyng notes, hye and clere,
Longe or the day[e]-rowes can a-pere, 54
  Ymagyny*n*g that sche be my p*ro*pre name
Me calde ande sayde : " A-wake & Ryse, for shame,

(9)

Oute of thy slombre-bed of slouth & sleep, 57
  Remembring the vpon this lusty seson "—

_{36 For] ffo.   40 mervell] merevell hit.   42 mery] *om*.}

4   I. *The Nightingale's Song in Aurora, Prime, Tierce.*

<small>I rose</small>

<small>and went on till I found her singing and sitting on a green laurel.</small>

<small>Putting all worldly thoughts out of my heart,</small>

<small>I understood at last that she was singing of her coming death.</small>

<small>So she sang in 'Aurora,'</small>

<small>and continued doing so in 'Prime,'</small>

<small>[leaf 60]</small>
<small>in 'Tierce,'</small>

Ande right with that oute of my bed y leep,
Thenking in my conceyt, she seide me reson,
Ande walked forth—she yaf me gret encheson—   61
Til that y come ther as my hertis queene
Ryght freshly sang vpon a laurer grene.   63

(10)
Entendyng, as y romed vp and dou*n*,   64
Expelling clerly all wilfle negligence,
Hir clere entoned notes and hir sou*n*
For to p*er*ceyue with all my diligence,
And sodenly co*n*ceyued y this sentence,   68
Hough that this brid, a-mong hir notes glade,
Right of hir deth a note of mornyng made.   70

(11)
Ande in Aurora, that is the morowe gray,   71
Ascending vp into this tre full hye,
Me thoght she syngyng sayd this same day:
"For all my myrthes ande my melodye,
As nature will, about none shall y dye.   75
My curio*us* note ne shall noght me a-vayle,
But mortall deth me sharply will a-saile."   77

(12)
Contynving so vnto the oure of prime,   78
Vpon the *bogh she euer sat and songe,
But, dou*n* descendyng, she sayde in hasti tyme:
"My lyfe be kynde endure shall not longe."
But notheles thorgh-oute the wode yt ronge—   82
Hir notes clere—so merily ande so shryll,
The wych enchesoned me tabide there styll,   84

(13)
Till that hyt drogh forther of the day,   85
Aboute the oure of tierce, right as y gesse,
That euer y-lyke with notes fresh ande gay
She cesed not, whech y can not expresse
So delitable, replet with all swetnesse,   89

<small>59. 63 right] rygh.   63 laurer] laureall.   65 clerly] clerkely.
71 is] *om*.   75 will] woll.   76 noght me] me noght.   79 bogh] boght c.   81 endure shall] enduryth.   82 thorgh-oute] thorght-oute.   83 merily] mery.   84 there] *om*.   85 that] *om*.   forther] ffethyre.</small>

I. *The Nightingale dies. Her story is in a Latin book.* 5

But euer among she song: "Ocy, ocy,"
Whech signified, me thoght, that she shuld dye.

(14)
Ande aftir this, when Phebus in his spere   92
 Ouer all the world had sprad his bemes bright,
Cavsynge the cloudes dym for to be clere,
Ande derk[e] mystes enlumyned with his lyght,
Aboute the oure of sixt then she a-lyght   96   and in
 Ande singynge seet in myddes of the tre: 'Sexte.'
"Ocy, Ocy, o deth, well-come to me!"   98

(15)
Thus, fro the morowe *to myddes of the day   99
Ande all the nyght a-fore, with open eye,
This bryd hath songen, as ye haue herd me say,
Rehersyng euery tyde with melodie,
But at the last, she shright—and sodenlye,   103   At last, in
 Hir songe, hir myrth, & melodye was done   the evening,
Ande she expyred aboute the oure of none.   105   at 'Nones,'
                                                       she died.

(16)
This brid, of whom y haue to you rehersed,   106
 Whych in her song expired thus ande deyede,
In latyn fonde y in a boke well versed,   This story I
 Ande what in morall sense it signifiede,   found in a
                                                       Latin book,
                                                       and under-
The whech in englysh y wold were notified   110   took to trans-
 To all that lusty are it for to here,   late it.
Yf that my conny[n]ge suffycyent ther-to were.

(17)
Be this nyghtingale, that thus freshly can   113   It is an alle-
 Bothe wake and singe, as telleth vs scripture,   gory of the
                                                       Christian
Is Crist hym-self ande euery cristen-man   soul,
 Soule vnderstande, whech oweth of nature   which ought
                                                       always to
 Ande verray reson do diligence ande cure,   117   bear in mind
 Oute of the sleep of synne to a-wake, & ryse,   the passion of
                                                       our Lord as
                                                       a remedy for
 Ande to remembre, ande fully aduertise,   119   a man's sin.

90 song] schange.   95 enlumyned] enlewmyde.   96 sixt] vj.
97 seet] sate.   99 to] to the c.C.   106 of] to.   111 To all]
Toull ull.   lusty] *a preceding* are *blotted out* c.   112 conny[n]ge]
conynge.   115 cristen-man] kyrsteñ manes.   118 a-wake]
wake.

6   I. By Aurora, understand the Creation and Adam's fall.

(18)

[leaf 60, bk.] That be Aurora is vnderstonden right 120
By 'Aurora,' understand the creation of the world,
    The first begynny[n]g of this world of noght,
Ande how grete god, of his endles myght,
Hath heven ande yerth formed with a thoght,
And in six dayes all oder thynges wroght, 124

and how, for pride, Lucifer was cast down into Hell.
    Ande hogh gret nou*m*bre of angels bright & clere
Fell dou*n* for pride to helle with Lucifere. 126

(19)

Therefore man ought to be humble.
*Hygh or lowe, wheder-so-euer thow be, 127
    Enprinte that fall right my*n*dely in thy hert
Ande arme the surely with humylite
Ayen all pr*i*de, yf thou wylt lyue in *quert!
Saue thy soule, or elles shalt thou smerte 131
    For all thy wor[l]dly pr*i*de ande veyne desyre,
Ande euer in hell be brent with endles fyre! 133

(20)

In this hour, Adam and Eve sinned by envy:
Muse on this morow further, and conceyue 134
    How that oure fader Adam ande also Eue,
Whom that the sotell serpent can deceyue
Of pure envye and caused to mischeue,—
Ande let theyr smert thi herte perse & cleue : 138

we are still under the curse of their misdoing,
Thenk well that fall is to thi-self extended
Ande, nade Crist died, it had not yit be amended!

(21)

and, without Christ's mercy, should be separated from God,
Before whos deth the gret Infyrmyte 141
    Of that offens, cleped originall,
Thorogh-oute the world infecte had vch de-gre,
That, when they deyed, streyght to hell went all,
*Tyll fro the trone a-bofe celestyall 145
    Crist, consyderyng the gret captyuyte
Of all man-kynde, cam *doune of pure pite. 147

(22)

as Adam was driven from Paradise.
This hygh forfet whych Adam sone had don 148
    Was grounde & cause of oure mortalite

121 begynny[n]g] begynnynge.   world] worde.   124 six] vj.
127 Hygh] Hyght c.   128 fall] schall.   129 the] the rygh.
130 quert] quarte c.   131 Saue] Safe so.   smerte] semrt.   132 wor[l]dly] worldely.   139 thi-self] they-selfe.   140 amended] me*n*dyt.   143 Thorogh-oute] Throgh-oute.   145 Tyll] Thyll c.   a-bofe] Aboue (*blotted out*) abofe.   147 doune] dom c.

I. *Think on thy poor birth and thy vicious life.*

And paradise made hym for to voide *Anone :
Oo sely appell, so eten of a tre !
O welthy pepyll, in *your* prosperite 152
   Thenk euery morowe how þat *your* wor[l]dly wele
   More lykly ys, safe grace, to hyrt then hele ! 154

(23)

Ande in Aurora further to procede, 155   [leaf 61]
  Be-thenke thy-self, hough porely þu was born   Do not forget thy birth in poor estate.
Ande, as kynde will, *þu nedes mvst succede
  In pyne ande wo, lyke other the be-forn :
  Deth cometh in hast, he will not be for-born, 159   Death may suddenly slay thee.
   For in the oure of thy natiuite
   He entered first & manaced the to sle. 161

(24)

In-to the wor[l]de what hast thou broght wit*h* the 162
  But lamentacioñ, wepyng, woo, & crye ?
Non other richesse, safe only lyberte,
  With which god hath endowed the richly,
  Ande byddeth the frely chese to lyue or dye : 166   By thy own free will thou mayst live or die for ever.
   Fro one of tho ne shall thou not deseuer,
   In Ioie or wo to liue or dye for euer. 168

(25)

Be nothyng prowde thy byrth thus to remembre, 169   Every morrow remember the sins of thy youth,
  Thou hast thy youth dispended folilye,
Ande vsest with othes gret thy lord dismenbre,
  Ande other-wyse yit lyuest thou viciously.
  Call to thy mynde these thinges by & by, 173   and pray to God for remission.
   And euery morowe, thogh thou lust to sleep
   Ande softly lye, a-wake, a-ryse, and wep ! 175

(26)

But, forther to declare in speciall 176   In this very same hour
  This oure of morowe, yf þat y con*n*yng hade,
Ande hogh this brid thus song with voice mortall
  Ande in hire song a note of mornyng made,

---

150 Anone] or none c. 153 wor[l]dly] worldly. 154 More] e *above the line* c. 155 Ande] An. 156/7 þu] u *above the line* c. 156 þu] *follows erasure* c. 157 þu nedes mvst] þu nedest mvst c ; thou moste nede C. 159 will] woll. 162 wor[l]de] world. 165 With] *a preceding* Wh *blotted out* c ; Wit*h* the C. 166 byddeth the] by the. 167 shall] schalt. 171 lord] lorld. 172 thou] *om.* 173 these] this. 177 yf] ycf.

8   I. *Remember Christ's death, and at Prime, Noah's Flood.*

    Konnyng and langage in me are so fade,   180
      That nedes y mvst in hvmble wyse exhort
      You that are konning, with pacience me supporte.

(27)

    Oure lorde Ihe*s*us, the fadres sapiens,   183
      The well of trewth & sothfastnes diuine,
      The lombe vnspotted, the grounde of Innocence,
      That gyltles for oure gylt lust to declyne,

Christ was betrayed, and taken prisoner by the Jews.

    This oure of morow, cleped matutyne,   187
      Falsly be-trayed, and with þe Iewes taken,
      And of hys o[w]ne disciples sone for-saken :   189

(28)

[leaf 61, bk.]
Never forget His humble suffering;

    O synfull man, this oure the aght remord,   190
      That standest exiled oute fro charite,
      To thenke howe that thy maker & thy lord
      So lowly suffred this reprefe for the,
    Yevyng the ensample, that with humilite   194

and do thy best to follow His example.

      Fro morow to nyght thou folow shuld his trace,
      Yf thou in heuen with hym wilt cleyme a place.

(29)

    Fro morow to nyght be-tokenes All the tyme,   197
      Syth thou wast born streyght tyll þat thou dye.
      Thus endyth the first oure and now to pr*i*me.

In 'Prime'

      Ande be this oure, what we may sygnifie,
      In whych this brid thus songe with melodie,   201
      The seconde age ys clerly notyfied

the Flood broke in,

    When all the world with water was destryed,   203

(30)

and only Noah, with seven fellows, was saved, whereas all other people perished.

    In tyme of Noe whom for hys ryghtwisnesse,   204
      And with hym seuen, all-myghty god reserued ;
      And elles all oder for synne ande wrechednesse,
      Of verey rygo*u*r, ryght as thay had deserued,
    In that gret flood were dreynt and ouer-terved.   208
      Except viij soules, all perysched, lesse and more,
      And they preserued, this world for to restore.   210

    188 Iewes] ywes.   189 o[w]ne] oune.   195 nyght] nygh.
    196 Yf] Yeff.   198 wast] were.   201 thus] *om.*   202 age] *om.*
    210 for] *om.*

I. *Think how Christ bought thee with His blood.* 9

(31)
This oure, to thenke that with the water wan 211
Noght all the world was ouerflow for synne,
Aught for to exite euery maner man,
  That vice ande vertu can discerne a-twynne, *Therefore eschew sin,*
  All vice to eschew and vertuosly be-gynne 215 *and live virtuously.*
    Oure lord to plese, thenkyng furthermore,
    He *hateth synne now as he dud be-fore, 217

(32)
Thagh that hym lust of mercy and pite, 218 *God is not hasty to take vengeance;*
  As for a tyme, his vengance to differre,
Sith with hys precious blod vpon a tre
  Hath boght oure soules—was neuer thyng boght derre :—
    *Ley to thy sore, & let no-thyng lye nerre 222
    Then this same salfe, to hele with thy smert : *He rather likes a penitent sinner.*
    Full glad ys he, when so thou wilt conuert. 224

(33)
For of the synner the deth he not desireth, 225 [leaf 62]
  But that he wold retorne to lyfe a-yeyn.
For, whosoeuer in dedly synne expyreth, *If thou die in deadly sin, thou forfeitest pardon.*
  Ther is no pardon that may abregge his payne.
    This to remembre aught cause the to restreyne 229
    Fro euery synne þat wyll this lord displese
    And for to vse that hym may queme & plese. 231

(34)
Ande on this oure to thenke furthermore, 232
  When all the flood *aswaged was and cesed,
They, not considryng the gret vengaunce afore,
  The seed of Noe, whych gretly was encresed, *Noah's posterity soon forgot God's judgment, and turned to evil;*
  But vn-to vice on vch syde ran and pressed, 236
    For which they pvniched were with plages sore,
    As in the byble more pleynly may ye here. 238

(35)
O thow, that hast thus past the oure of morow 239 *but thou, advanced in life,*
  Ande newly entrest in *the oure of prime,

212 Noght] How.   214 a-twynne] Atweñ.   217 hateth] hatheth c; hatetht C.   be-fore] Aforne.   220 vpon] Appoñ. 222 Ley] Ley that c.   223 with] with All.   233 aswaged was] was aswaged c.   236 vn-to] in-to.   240 newly] *follows erasure* c. in] in-to.   the oure] thoure c.

beware of the sins of thy forefathers and the attacks of the Fiend.	Aught to be war to here of woo and sorow
	  Which in this worlde hath be a-fore thy tyme,
	And of the fend, that *redy is to lyme 243
	  Thy soule wyth synne & cach the in his snare,
	Yif he in vertu the bareyne fynde and bare. 245

(36)

God has protected thee, as a youth, against evil;	Ande namely now, sith thou of Innocence 246
	  Ande of thy tendre age art past the yeres,
	In which god the hath keept fro violence,
	  In all thy youth fro Sathan and his feres,

now do it thyself with the help of Christ,	Dispose the nowe to sadnes and prayeres, 250 Remembryng specially vpon this oure of prime, Hogh Crist acused falsly was of Cryme, 252

(37)

who, in this hour, was led before Pilate,	Taken ande lad afore the presydent, 253
	  Pounce Pylat, that Iuge was of the lawe,
	His handes bounde, his nek with boffettes bent,
	  On euery syde to-togged and to-drawe.

and there suffered much from the Jews.	He, ffull *of pacience, suffred all & sawe 257 Hogh that the Iewes, fals and voide of grace, There all defouled with spet his blessed face. 259

(38)

[leaf 62, bk.] All these pains He endured	Se, hogh this lord that all thing made of noght, 260
	  To saue mannes soule, wold suffre this repref,
	That myght haue staunched & cesede with a thoght
	  The Iewes malice & put theym to myscheef,

to give us an example of patience.	To oure ensample, þat we shuld suffre grefe 264 Aftir oure desert and paciently hit take For hym that all wolde suffre for oure sake. 266

(39)

Young gallants, remember this hour against the attacks of wantonness.	O lusty gaylauntes in youre adolescens, 267
	  Let not this oure of prime fro you deseuer!
	When ye be sterede to wanton in-solence,
	  *Restreyne your-self & in your herte thenk euer

Solomon warns you.	How Salomon sayde; he cowde perceyve neuer 271

243 redy is] ys redy the c.   247 the] thi.   248 the hath] hathe the.   253 afore] before.   257 of] of pite & c.   263 theym] them.   266 all wolde] wolde all.   269 be] beñ.   270 Restreyne] Restreyned c.   271 Salomon] Saloman.

I. *At Tierce, dread God's judgment on Sodom's crime.* 11

The waunton weyes & dyuers of your youth,
For all the prudent wisdom that he *kowthe! 273

(40)
Thoure of pryme fynysched thus & ended, 274
This brid all-wey perseuereth ande a-byt,
Doun on the tre a-valed and descended,
Thoure of tierce clerely syngyng yit.
The third age of the world be-tokeneth hyt, 278
In whech thoo folk that doun fro Noe came
Gretly encresed in tyme of Abraham, 280

In 'Tierce' the nightingale sang of Abraham,

(41)
Which in his daies perfit was ande stable, 281
Dredyng oure lord and lyuyng perfytly;
*To whom god swore, lik sterres in-nvmerable
His seed he wolde encrese and multiplie.
But, notheles, moch peple viciously 285
Were in this age dampnably demeyned
Ande thorgh theire vice destreied sore & steyned.

who led a goodly life, and received God's promise;

but, also in his time, many people did not mend their bad behaviour:

(42)
Their filthi synne abhominable stank 288
Ande so displesed the blessed Trinite,
That doun to hell sodenly ther sank
Sodom, ande Gomor, and oder cites thre,
Ande now is there but the Ded[e] See. 292
Alas the while that euer they wolde do so!
Vnkyndly synne was cause of all their woo. 294

God could not let them be unpunished;

so Sodom and Gomorrah were destroyed.

(43)
This for to here aght cause your herte to colde, 295
That are enprinted aftyr the ymage
Of god, and to considere and be-holde
This gret vengaunce, taken in þat age.
And namely ye that are in the third age 299
Of your lyfe ande passed morow & prime,
Aght euer be war to vse vnkyndly crime. 301

People, in their later years, ought to be warned by this terrible end,

and leave off sin.

---

273 kowthe] kowde c; koude C.   277 syngyng] syngnified.
279 In] *follows erasure* c.   280 in] *om.*   283 To] The c.   287 destreied] desteied.   292 is there] ther is.   299 *and* 300 *transposed in* C.   301 euer] *follows erasure* c.

12   I. *The Fiend lies in wait for you. Death knocks at your Gate.*

(44)

[leaf 63]
The Fiend
always tries
to catch
souls;

The fende, youre enmye, lying in a-wayte, 302
   Goth fast a-boute, your soules to deceyue,
   Leying hys lynes and with mony a bayte
   Wsynge his hokes, on theym you to receyue,

but Christ's
sufferings
make us able
to avoid the
Devil's
snares.

The which thus lygh[t]ly ye may eschewe & weyfe,
   This oure to thenk hogh Iewes lowde and hye
   Gan : "Crucifige, crucifige !" Crye, 308

(45)

For our sake
the Jews
forced Him

Takyng oure lord and, of derisioun, 309
   In cloth of purpull clothing hym in scorne,
   Ledynge hym forth, as childre of confusioun,
   And on his heed a sharpe croun set of thorñ ;

to bear the
cross to
Calvary.

Vpon his blessed shulder the crosse was borñ 313
   Vnto the place of *peynes, Caluarie :
      Lo, what he suffred, thi soule fro peyne to bye !

(46)

Thenk on this oure, thou wrecched synfull man, 316
   That in this age hast reson, strenght, and hele,
   (Yf thou asayled or hurt be with Sathan),
   To salf thy sore and thi wonde to hele :

Christ suf-
fered all this
to give thee
defences
against the
attacks of
Satan.

Mark in thi mynde this oure for woo or wele, 320
   Hogh that thy lord suffred for thy gylt,
      To saue thy soule, whech elles had be spilt. 322

(47)

Lords, be
watchful,

Ye myghty prynces and lordes of a-state, 323
   In honoure here that are exalted hye,

Death may
come on a
sudden.

Beth ware & wake, deth knokketh at your yate
   And woll come in ; be sure that ye shall dye !
   Call to your mynde for speciall remedie 327
      Oure lordes passioñ, his peyne, & pacience
      As medycyne chefe & shelde of all defence. 329

(48)

A myghty prince, lusty, yonge, & fiers, 330
   Amonge the peple sore lamented ys :

302 youre] oure.   305 Wsynge] *the first letter not clear
neither in* c *nor in* C.   306 lygh[t]ly] lyghtly.   314 Vnto]
Vpoñ.   peynes] peynes, calde c.   323 Ye] The.   325 Beth]
Byth.   328 peyne] pyme.   331 peple] pepull that.

I. *The Duke of Warwick is dead. Why please the Devil?*

The duc of Warwyk; entryng the oure of tierce
Deth toke hym to whom mony sore shall mysse.
All-myghty Ihesu, receyue his soule to blisse! 334
Both hye & lowe, thenk well that ye shall henne,
Deth wyll you trise, ye wot not how ne whenne.

In the 'Tierce' of his life, the Duke of Warwick was taken away.

(49)
Aftir the oure of tierce this nyghtyngale, 337
Synging euer with notes fresh and gay,
To myddes of this tre can doun *avale,
When that yt drogh to myddes of the day:
Sygnyfinge all the tydes, soth to say, 341
Whech that haue be fro tierce vnto syxt.
In which dayes, whoso woll rede the tyxt 343

From 'Tierce' till 'Sexte,' the nightingale continued singing.

(50)
Of the byble, he may haue revth to here 344 [leaf 63, bk.]
Hogh dampnably in mony a sondry place
Of the world that folk demeyned were,
Destryed for synne and destitute of grace.
O synfle Dathan, the yerth *in lytyll space 348
Opened & swolowed bothe the and Abyron,
And sodenly with yow sank mony a synfle moñ.

In this hour Dathan and Abiram were swallowed by the earth;

(51)
Lo, in all ages, be freelte of nature, 351
Thorgh all the world peple hath had delite
The fend to serue with all theire besy cure,
Which for theire seruyce no-thyng wil hem quite
But endles deth. Allas, what appetite 355
Haue folkes blynde, such a lord to plese,
That noght rewardeth but myscheef & desese. 357

for people always liked to be bondsmen to the Devil, though he is but an ungracious master.

(52)
And in speciall, ye of perfyt age, 358
This oure of sixt, in myddes of your lyfe,
Aught to be war and wayte aftir þe wage
That Crist rewardeth with-oute werre or stryfe,
Wher endles Ioye and blysse are euer ryfe. 362

In the middle of their lives people ought to look for the mercy of Christ,

332 Warwyk] Warre.   333 hym to] to hym.   336 wyll] woll.
339 avale] a-vaile c.   343 woll] wyll.   345 dampnably] dampnable.   348 in] in a c.   349 &] an.   354 for] ofor, or *partly erased*.   hem] theym.

14 I. At Sexte and Nones, think of Christ's Cross and Death.

   Entendeth duly this blessed lord to serue,
   That, you to saue, vpon the rode wolde sterve. 364

(53)

who was crucified, innocent as a lamb.

  Vnto the crosse, thoure of syxte, was nayled   365
   Oure lord Ihesus, hangyng ther with theves,
  And for the thrist of tormentes, that hym ailed,
   Eysell and gall in scornes and repreues   368
  They offred hym—oure crym & olde mescheues,—
   Doyng a-way this lambe thus crucified :
  The manhed suffred, the godhed neuer died.   371

(54)

We must never forget the pains He suffered,

  We aght *ryght well compassioñ haue & reuth,   372
   For to remenbre his peynes and repreues,
  To thenk, hogh he whych grounde is of [all] trewth

hanging between two thieves.

   Was demed to hange amyd to fals[e] theues.
  O blessed lord and leche to all oure greues,   376
   So of thy grace graunt vs to be so kynde,
  To haue this oure of sixt well in oure mynde.   378

(55)

[leaf 64] From the 6th to the 9th hour Christ was hanging on the cross.

  Thus heng oure lord nayled to the tre,   379
   Fro the oure of sixt vnto *the oure of none,—
  Ande also longe was in prosperite
   Oure fader Adam, tyll tyme that he had doñ

Adam was in prosperity, till, by his fall, he was banished into the earth;

  That high forfet for which he banyshid sone   383
   Was *in-to yerth, to lyue in langour there
  Ande all his o[f]spryng,—till Longens with a spere,

(56)

  The oure of none, as Iewes hym desyred,   386
   Thirled and persed thorgh his hert & side.

Christ died,

  He, seyng then : " Consummatum est," expired

His soul went to His Father.

   And heed enclyned, the gost yaf vp þat tyde
  Vnto the fader. The sunne, compelled to hyde   390
   His bemys bright, no lenger *myght endure
  To see the deth of the auctor of nature.   392

---

  365 crosse] +. 367 the] *follows erasure* c. thrist] stryfe.
ailed] inled. 369 crym] tyme. 372 ryght] ryth c. &] *follows erasure* c. 374 he] *follows erasure* c. all] *om.* c. 375 to] ij.
378 sixt] vj^te. 380 vnto] in-to. the oure] thoure c. 383 banyshid] banehed. 384 in-to] in-te c. 385 all] Allso. 386 Iewes] ywes. 387 thorgh] thorghoute. 391 myght] myth c.

I. *He has bought us, & slain Death. May He grant us Heaven!* 15

(57)

Thus hath this brid, thus hath this nyghtyngale, 393
  Thus hath this blessed lord þat all hath wroght,
That dou*n* to yerth fro heuen can a-vale,
  Vpon a crosse oure soules dere y-bought
Ande yeuen vs cause in hert, wyll, & thought, 397   Let us thank Him, that He
  Hym for to serue & euer loue and drede   shed His
That, vs to saue, wold suffre his blod to shede.   blood for our sake.

(58)

Hell despoiled, & slayn oure mortall foo, 400   After our Lord's resur-
  Oure lord vpryse with palme of hye victorie,   rection and ascension,
Ascended eke ayen there he come fro,
  The holy gost sent from the see of glory   the Holy Ghost sent
  His precious body to vs in memory, 404   us the Sacra-ment of the
    With holy wordes of dewe *con*secraciou*n*   Altar.
    To be receyued to oure hele & sauaciou*n*. 406

(59)

Who may be glad but all thoo, at lest, 407   All those may be glad who
  That worthy are, in this lyues space,   are worthy to appear be-
For to be fed here, at this glorious fest,   fore Christ's face, both
  Ande after, in heuen, wit*h* bryghtnes of his face,   here and in heaven.
  Whom of his godhed be-seche we ande his grace, 411   Let us pray that we may
    That, fro this worlde when so we shall deseuer,   have part in eternal life.
    In Ioye eternall with hym ther to pe*r*seuer.
Amen. . ; . 413

Explicit.

394 this] oure.   399 to shede] *illegible*.   402 come] came.
406 sauaciou*n*] saluacyou*n*.   407 at] at the.   409 glorious] *a following* ste *blotted out* c.

II.

A Sayenge of the Nyghtyngale.[1]

[By DAN JOHN LYGDATE: see p. 28.]

[54 stanzas of sevens, *ababbcc*.]

[*MS. Harl.* 2251, *leaf* 229 *a.*]

(1)

<small>On a lovely day in June,</small>

IN June, whan Titan was in Crabbes hede,   1
Towardes Even the Saphyre-huwed sky
Was westward meynt with many Rowes Rede,

<small>when the birds had just finished their even-song,</small>

And fowlis syngen [in] theyr melody
An hevenly complyne with sugred Armonye,   5
As *that hem nature taught[e] for the best :

<small>and gone to rest,</small>

They gan hem proygne and drough hem to theyr
[Rest—

(2)

That sith the tyme, forsoth, that j was borne,   8
Hadde j nat herd suche song in downe nor daale—
And alle were gone, sauf vpon a thorne
The same tyme j herd a nyghtyngale,

<small>I was lying in a valley and listening to the tunes of a nightingale.</small>

So as j lay pensyf in a vale   12
To herken the meanyng of hir melody,
Whos hertly refreyd was eue*r* : "Occy, occy."   14

(3)

<small>I understood that she was asking Venus for vengeance on false lovers :</small>

She ment, I trowe, with hir notes nuwe   15
And in hir *ledne, **Venus** to take vengeaunce
On false lovers whiche that bien vntriewe,
Ay ful of chaunge and of variaunce,
And can in oone to have no plesaunce.   19
This bridde ay song : "O sle theym, lady myn,
Withouten mercy and bryng hem to theyr fyn, 21

---

[1] In John Stowe's hand.   1 2nd in] in y^e.   3 westward] estwarde.   4 in] *om.* H.   5 complyne] cemplygne.   6 that hem] hem that H ; þat them A.   taught[e]] taught tho.   7 hem] them.   drough] drought.   9 nor] ne.   14 refreyd] refrayde. Occy, occy] ocylocy.   16 ledne] ledne on H A.   **Venus**] venis ; *proper names in heavy type are underlined in* H.   20 sle] sleth. 21 hem] them.

II. *I dream that an Angel from God comes to me.*

(4)

To shewe ensample, that other may wele knowe   22
How that they shal in theyr trowth abyde!
For parde, lady, yit thy sones bowe
Nys nat broke, whiche callid is Cupide.
Let hym marke them and wounde hem in the side   *Cupid should*
   Withouten mercye or any remedye,   *wound them with his*
   Where-so that he suche falsehede can espye. 28   *arrows;*

(5)

And suche as bien for love langwisshyng,   29   *but true*
   Cherissh hem, lady, for trewe affectiouñ,   *lovers should be helped.*
Support and help hem with thy myght to bryng
In-to thi Castell, sette in Citheroñ:
On dyamauñdes sette is the Dungeouñ,   33
   Fret with Rubyes and Emerawdes grene.
   Now herkne my song, that art of love the qwene!"   [leaf 229, bk.]

(6)

And as I lay, and herde hir twnes cliere,   36   *Taking great delight in the bird's song,*
   And on hir notes me gretely gan delite,
Vpon the Eve the sterris dide appere,
The bawmy vapour of grassis gan vp-smyte
In-to myn hede of floures Rede and white,   40
   That with the odour, or that I toke kepe,
   I fille anon in-to a dedly sleepe.   42   *I fell asleep.*

(7)

And than me sempte that from the god of love   43   *I dreamed that an angel from Heaven*
   To me was sent an vnkouth messangier—
Nought from Cupide, but fro the lord above—
   And, as me thought, ful fayre and fressh of chiere,
Whiche to me sayde: 'Foole, what dostow here   47   *summoned me,*
   Slepyng allone, gapyng vpon the mone?
   Rise, folowe me, [and] thow shalt se right sone   49

23 theyr] hur.   24 parde] pardy.   25 Nys nat] Is not.
26 hem] them.   27 Withouten] *with*-out.   28 falsehede] fallsed.
29 bien] be.   30 hem] them.   affectiouñ] affectyons.   31 hem] them.   40 hede] heued.   41 or] er.   42 fille] fell.   43 that] *om.* of love] *corrected out of:* above, *but by the same scribe* H; of loue A.   45 Nought] not.   fro] from.   47 dostow] dost thou.
49 and] *om.* H.

NIGHTINGALE.

18 II. *The Angel is to teach me the Nightingale's meaning.*

(8)

An vnkowth sight, If thow list to speede.   50
The briddes song I shal to the vnclose,
For trust me wele, I cast the nat to leede
Nothyng towardes the gardyn of the Rose,
And I thi spirit shal otherwise dispose,   54
  For to declare the briddis song : " Occy,"
  And what she meanyth in sentence triew[e]ly. 56

(9)

Thyn aduertence is gouerned wrong   57
Towchyng the twnes thow herdest here to-forne :
"Occy, occy," this was the briddis song,
Whiche many a lover hath thurgh foly lorne.
But thynk among vpon the sharp[e] thorne   61
  Whiche priked hir brest with *fyry remembraunce,
  Lovers in vertu to encres and avaunce.   63

(10)

This briddis song, whiche we have on honde—   64
Who that takith the moralite—
Betokenyth, playnly for to vndrestonde,
The grete fraunchise, the grete liberte,
Whiche shuld in love be so pure and fre,   68
  Of triewe meanyng Rooted so withynne,
  Fer from the conceyte of any maner synne.   70

(11)

*Takestow none heede, how this bridde so smal   71
Syngeth as that she wold hir-self dismembre,
Streyneth hir throte, peyneth hir brest at al,
Shakith and qwakyth in euery Ioynt and membre?
O man vnkynde, why dostow nat Remembre   75
  Among in hert vnto this briddes song?
  If thow advert,—thow dost to god grete wrong.

(12)

Thow art desseued in thyn oppyniouñ   78
And al awrong also thow dost goo,

Side notes:
to teach me the true meaning of the nightingale's singing,
because I had not interpreted it in the right way:
'She praises pure love, [leaf 230]
free from any sinful thought.
'She nearly kills herself with singing.
'This interpretation of thine

50 to] yᵉ. 58 twnes] toynes. herdest] haddest. 60 thurgh] thorugh. 62 priked] pricketh. fyry] fayre H. 63 to encres] tencresse them. 64 whiche] which yᵗ. 65 the] *om.* 66 Betokenyth] n *corrected out of* l H. 71 Takestow] Take thow H ; take thou A. 75 dostow] dost yᵘ.

II. *The bird shows folk Christ's sufferings for them.*

Feynt and vntriew thyne exposicioun, *is totally wrong;*
Thyn vndrestondyng, thy conceyt both[e] two.
This bridde, in soth, ne meanyth nothyng so : 82
For hir synggyng—who-so takith heede— *she does not sing of fleshly love,*
Nothyng Resownyth vnto flesshlyhede. 84

(13)
Towchyng: "Occy"—considre wele the woord!— 85 *but bewails the pains of our Lord,*
This brid it song of Impacience,
Of Iniuries doo vnto the lord
And wrong grete to his magnificence
Of worldly folk thurgh theyr grete offence, 89 *suffering for men's sins,*
Whiche can-nat knowe for theyr reklesnes
The grete love, the grete kyndenesse 91

(14)
Whiche he shewed for theyr *alre goode, 92 *who do not even care for His death on the cross.*
Whan that he, yif they kowde adverte,
For theyr sake starf vpon the Roode
And with a spere was stongen thurgh the hert:
Who felt euer for love so grete a smert 96
As thilk[e] lord dide for mannes sake?
And yit, allas, non hede therof they take. 98

(15)
To pay the Raunsoun of oure grete losse, 99
He was in love so gentil and so fre,
That hym deyned be nayled vpon the crosse [leaf 230, bk.]
And liche a thief hang vpon a tre.
Lift vp thyn hert, vnkynd man, *and see! 103 *'Day and night, the nightingale strives to make thee value Christ's kindness:*
The nyghtyngale in hir armonye
Thus day and nyght doth vpon the crye. 105

(16)
She cryeth: "Sle al tho that bien vnkynde 106 *"Slay all the ungrateful people who do not feel indebted to Christ,*
And can of love the custom nat observe,
Nor in theyr Ien no drope of pite fynde,
Nor in theyr brest, for love, no sigh conserve!
Why list the lord for mannes sake sterve 110

84 vnto] in-to. 87 Iniuries] iniures. doo] done. 89 folk] folkes. thurgh] thorugh. 90 reklesnes] rechellnesse. 92 alre] old H; ould A. 95 thurgh] thorugh. 96 smert] smarte. 98 take] toke. 99 Raunsoun] raunsome. 101 vpon] on. 103 and] at H. 106 tho] *om.* bien] be. 108 Ien] eghen.

II. Christ's wounds and death were foreseen by Isaiah.

<small>though He shed His blood for their salvation.</small>

But for to pay of fredam the Raunsoun̄,
His hert[e]-bloode, for theyr redempcioun̄ ?   112

(17)

<small>'Never forget His five wounds,</small>

His woundis fyve for man he did vnclose :   113
Of handis, of feete, and of his faire side.

<small>which are like a rose,</small>

Make of these fyve in thyn hert a Rose
And lete it there contynuauly abyde ;
Forgete hym nought, where thow go or ride,   117
Gadre on an hepe these rosen-floures fyve,
In thy memorye prynt hem al thy lyve :   119

(18)

<small>red with His blood.</small>

This is the Rose whiche first gan wexen rede,   120
Spreynt oueral with dropes of purpure hewe,
Whan Crist Ihesu was for mankynd dede
And had vpon̄ a garnement ful newe :   123

<small>"Like Mary, and Saint John,</small>

His holy moder, his Cousyn eke, seynt Iohn,
Suche array to-fore saugh they neuer none,   125

(19)

<small>every man ought to be touched to the utmost, to see Him endure such torments.</small>

Whiche to behold, god wote, they were nat fayne : 126
His blessyd body to seen so al to-Rent ;
A Crowne of thorn, that thrilled thurgh his brayne ;
And al the bloode of his body spent ;
His hevenly Ien, Allas, deth hath I-blent ;   130
Who myght, for Rowth, susteyne and behold
But that his hert of pite shuld cold !   132

(20)

<small>"Isaiah, when speaking of the 'man who [leaf 231] comes from Edom,' meant the same who was accused before Pilate.</small>

This was the same whiche that *Isaye   133
Saugh fro Edom come, with his cloth depeynt,
Steyned in Bosra ; eke dide hym aspye,
Bathed in bloode, til he gan woxen feynt ;
This is he that drank galle and eysel Imeynt ;
This is he that was afore Pilate atteynt   138
With false accusours in the consistorye,
Only to bryng mankynde to his glorye.   140

111 Raunsoun̄] raunsome.   115 in] of. Rose] voose.
117 hym] them. nought] not.   118 an] om. these] thos.
119 prynt] emprynt. hem] them.   123 garnement] garment.
125 neuer] nere. 128 thurgh] thorough. 130 Ien] egghen. 131 and] and to. 133 Isaye] I yow say H ; I you saye A. 134 fro] frome. come] cane. 136 gan] can. 137 galle and eysel] eysell and gall. 138 afore] to-fore. 139 accusours] accusers.

II. How Christ's disciples forsook Him, & the Jews tore Him.

(21)

He was most fayre founde in his stoole, 141
Walkyng of vertues with most multitude,
Blessyd, benyngne, and hevenly of his stoole,
Whiche with his suffraunce Sathan [can] conclude.
His humble deth dide the devil delude, 145
Whan he mankynd brought out of prisoun,
Makyng his fynaunce with his passioun. 147

"Through His humble death, the Lord vanquished Satan, and saved mankind.

(22)

Isaye, the most renomed prophete, 148
Axed of hym, why his garnement
Was rede and blody, ful of dropes wete—
So disguysed was his vestyment!—
Like hem that pressen quayers of entent 152
In the pressour, both the Rede *and white—
So was he pressid thy Raunsoun for to qwyte!—

"Asked, why Christ's garment was so red, Isaiah answers with the Saviour's own words:

(23)

'It is, quod he, that trade it al alone. 155
Withouten felawe I gan the wyne out-presse,
Whan on the crosse I made a doleful mone
And thurgh myn hert the sperhed gan it dresse—
Who felt euer so passyng grete duresse!— 159
Whan al my friendis allone me forsoke
And I my-self this Iourney on me tooke. 161

'Alone I pressed the wine in the press when I was suffering on the cross, forsaken by every man

(24)

Except my moder there durst none abide 162
Of my disciples, for to suwen me.
Seynt Iohn, for love, stode on myn other side,
Alle the Remenaunt from me diden flee.
The Iewes my flessh asonder dide *tee: 166
Who was it but I that bode in the vyne
To presse the wyne, thy Raunsoun for to fyne?

except Mary and Saint John.

'Through the cruelty of the Jews

144 can] *om.* H.   148 renomed] renoumed.   150 dropes] *a following* wem *blotted out* H.   152 hem] them.   quayers] quayers.   153 and] and the H.   154 Raunsoun] raunsome.   155 is] is I.   156 Withouten] With-out.   163 suwen] followe.   164 on] by.   165 from] fro.   diden flee] dyd wend.   166 tee] rend H A.   167 bode] abode.   168 presse the] presse out.   Raunsoun] raunsome.

II. *How Christ suffered in His five wits for man's sake.*

(25)

[leaf 231, bk.] For mannes sake with me ful hard it stoode : 169
  Forsaken of alle and eke disconsolate ;

I lost all My blood : They left no drope, but d[r]ewe out al my bloode.
  Was neuer none so poore in none estate !

but nobody showed mercy on My pains. Al my disciples left me desolate 173
  Vpon the crosse betwene theves tweyne
   And none abode to Rewe vpoñ my peyne. 175

(26)

  O ye al that passen bi the wey, 176
   Lift vp the Ie of yowre aduertence !

'Never did any man endure such torments as I. Sawe ye euer any man so deye
  Withouten gilt, that neuer dide offence ?
   Or is there any sorwe in existence 180
    Liche the sorwe that I dide endure,
    To bye mankynde, vnkynde creature ? 182

(27)

'In all My five senses I suffered for man's misdoings : For the surfete of thy synnes alle, 183
  And for the offence of thy wittes fyve
   My towche, my tast, myn heryng dide apalle,
    Smellyng and sight ful fieble were als blyve.
    Thus, in eche part that man can contryve, 187
     I suffred peyne and in euery membre
     That any man can reken or remembre. 189

(28)

  Ageyne the synnes plainly of thyn heede 190
   I had vpoñ a crowne of thornes kene,
    Bitter teres were medled with my brede—
    For mannes trespas I felt al the tene—

In sight, My Ien blynde, that whylom shoone so sheene, 194
  But for man, in my thurst most felle,
   I drank galle tempred with eyselle. 196

(29)

  For mannes lokyng fulfilled with outrage, 197
in taste,   And for his tunge ful of detractiouñ
  I alone souffred the damage,

171 d[r]ewe] drewe. 176 ye al] all ye. wey] wye. 177 Ie] eghe. 178 deye] dye. 183 surfete] forfeyte. 187 part] port. can] maye. 193 tene] teme. 194 My] myn. 195 But] and.

II. *Christ is the remedy against man's Seven Sins.*

And ageyne falsehed of adulacioun
 I drank galle poynaunt as poysoun; 201
  Ageyn *heringe of tales spoken in vayne   *in hearing,*
  I had rebuke and sayde no word ageyne. 203 [leaf 232]

(30)

Gey*n* pride of beawte, where-as folkes trespas, 204
 I suffred my-self grete aduersite:
Beten and bonched in myn owne face;
 Ageyns towchyng, if man list to se,   *in touch.*
 Myn handes were nayled fast vn-to the tre, 208
  And for mysfotyng, where men went[e] wrong,
  My feete thurgh-pe*r*ced: Were nat my peynes
   strong? 210

(31)

Was it nat I that trespassed nought, 211 '*Though without any sin, I suffered all this.*
 That had myn hert pe*r*ced even atweyne,
And neue*r* offendid oones in a thought,
 Yit was it korve thurgh in eue*r*y veyne?
 Who felt eue*r* in erth so grete a peyne, 215
  To Reken al, giltles as dide I?—
 Wherfor this brid sang ay: "Occy, occy."— 217

(32)

Suche as ben to me founde vnkynde 218 '*Those who have forgotten that My passion is a remedy*
 And have no mynd kyndly of resoun,
But of slowth have I-left behynde
 The holy remembraunce of my passioun,
 By meane of whiche and mediacioun 222 *against the seven sins,*
  Ageyne al poysoun of the synnes seven
  Triacle I brought, sent [them] downe from heven—

(33)

Ageyns pride, remembre my mekenesse; 225 *ought to remember My meekness against pride, My poverty against covetousness, My purity against lechery, My charity against envy, My 40 days' abstinence against gluttony.*'
 Geyne covetise, thynk on my pouerte;
Ageynst lecherye, thynk on my clennesse;
 Agenst envye, thynk on my charite;
 Agenst glotonye, aduerte in hert and se 229

202 Ageyn] Agaynst. heringe of tales] tales heryng H.
207 Ageyns] Agaynst. man] men. 208 handes] hande.
210 thurgh-] thorugh-. 213 oones] once. 214 korve] kevne.
thurgh] thorughe. 215 a] *om.* 221 holy] hole. 224 them]
om. H. 227 Ageynst] ageyne. 228. 229 Agenst] ageyns.

II. Christ gave His body and blood for man's food.

How that I for mannes grete offence
Fourty dayes lyved in abstynence.' 231

(34)

"Against pride He humbly inclined His head; against envy [leaf 232, bk.]
" Of mekenesse he dide his [heued] enclyne 232
   Agenst the synne and the vice of pride ;
Agenst envy, streyght out as a lyne,

He spread abroad His arms as a token of friendship;
Spradde his armes out on every side,
[To enbrace his frendes and with them abyde,] 236
   Shewyng hem signes, who so list to se :
Grounde of his peynes was perfite charite. 238

(35)

against covetousness the nails pierced His hands.
Agenst covetise mankynde to redresse 239
   Thurgh-nayled weren his holy handis tweyne,
Shewyng of fredam his bountevous almesse,
Whan he for love suffred so grete peyne
To make mankynde his blisse to atteyne ; 243

"From His largesse He gave
   And his largesse to Rekene by and by,
I shal reherse his gyftes ceriously. 245

(36)

to man His body in the form of bread,
He gaf his body to man for chief repast, 246
   Restoratif best in the forme of brede,
At his maunde, or he hennys past ;

His blood in the form of wine,
His blessid bloode, in forme of wyne so Rede ;
His soule in price, whan that he was dede ; 250

and water out of His side to wash away his sins.
And of oure synne as chief lauendere,
Out of his side he gaf vs water cliere. 252

(37)

"To the Jews He gave His garment;
He gaf also his purpure vestement 253
   To the Iewis, that dide hym crucifie ;

to the apostles His dead body;
To his apostels he gaf also of entent
His blissed body, ded whan he dide lye ;

to Saint John His mother, and to His father His soul.
And his moder, that clepid was **Marie**,— 257
   The kepyng of hir he gaf to seynt Iohn̄ ;
And to his fader his gost, whan he was gon. 259

---

230 grete] *om.* 232 heued] *om.* H. 236 *om.* H. 237 hem] them. 240 Thurgh-] thorugh-. 241 his] a. 248 maunde] maundy. hennys] hence. 249 so] full. 251 synne] synnes. 253 purpure] 1st r *above the line* H. 254 dide hym] him did. 255 also] eke. 259 he] hit.

(38)

Agenst slowth he shewed grete doctryne,	260	"Against slowness He
Whan he hym hasted toward his passiouñ;		showed readiness to His passion,
Agenst wrath this was his disciplyne,		against
Whan he was brought to examynaciouñ:		wrath, meekness before
A soft Aunswere without rebelliouñ;	264	His judges;
Agenst glotenye he drank eysel and galle,		against gluttony He
To oppresse surfayte of vicious folkes alle.	266	drank gall and vinegar

(39)

He gaf also a ful grete remedye	267	
To mankynde, his sores for to sounde,		
For, ageyne the hete of lecherye,		against lechery He
Mekely he suffred many a grevous wounde,		[leaf 233]
For none hole skynne was in his body founde,	271	suffered many wounds.
Nor ther was seyn other apparaile,		
But bloode, allas, aboute his sides rayle.	273	

(40)

There he was sone and his faders heyre,	274	
With hym allone by the eternyte:		
It was a thyng incomparable fayre,		"It was a most wonderful thing that
The sone to dye, to make his seruaunt free,		God slew His
Hym fraunchisyng with suche liberte,	278	only Son to save mankind.
To make man, that was thurgh synne thralle,		
The court to enherite above celestial.	280	

(41)

These kyndenesses, whiche I to the Reherse,	281	"Never forget this exceeding
Lete hym devoyde from the[e] oblyvioun		kindness.
And lete the nayles, whiche thurgh his feete dide perce,		
Be a cliere myrrour for thy redempciouñ;		
Enarme thy-self for thy proteccioñ,	285	"Arm thyself against the
Whan that the feendis list ageyn the stryve,		attacks of the devils
With the Carectes of his wondes fyve.	287	with the signs of Christ's wounds.

(42)

Agenst theyr malice be strong and wele ware,	288	"Take His cross as
Al of his crosse Reyse vp the banner		thy banner;

266 surfayte] sourfetes.   268 his] ther.   272 seyn] sene no.
273 rayle] ryall.   279 thurgh] thorugh.   281 These] thos.
kyndenesses] kyndnes.   282 hym] them.   the[e] om.   283
thurgh] thorugh.   284 a] om.   for] of.   redempciouñ] dedemcyon.   286 ageyn] agaynst.   287 Caractes] correctes.   288
Agenst] Agayne.   289 Reyse] aryse.

II. Christ's Cross is typified by Old-Testament symbols.

  And thynk how he to Caluarye it bare,
   To make the strong agenst theyr daungier;
   Whiche whan they seen, they dare com no nere, 292

it is the best weapon:
   For trust wele, his crosse is best defence
    Agenst the power of fiendes violence.   294

(43)

It is the palm of victory;
  It is the palme, as clerkis can wele telle,   295
   To man in erth to conquest and victorye;

the tree of Daniel;
  It is the tre, whiche that **Danyell**
   Sawe sprad so broode, as made is memorye;

the key of Heaven; the staff of James;
  The key of heven, to bryng men to glorye;   299
   The staf of **Iacob**, causyng al oure grace,
   With whiche that he Iowrdan dide passe;   301

(44)

the ladder of our ascen- [leaf 233, bk.] *sion; the hook of Leviathan; the press of our redemption;*
  Scale and ladder of oure *ascencyon;   302
   Hooke and snare of the **Leviathan**;
  The strong pressour of oure Redempcioun,
   On whiche the bloode downe be his sides Ranne,
   For nothyng ellis, but for to save man;   306
   The harp of **Dauid**, whiche most myght availe,

the harp of David;
   Whan that the fiend kyng **Saul** dide assaile.

(45)

the pole whereon Moses exhibited the brazen serpent;
  This was the poole and the hygh[e] tree,   309
   Whilom sette vp by **Moyses** of entent—
  Al **Israel** beholde nygh and see—
   And therevpon of brasse a grete se*r*pent,
   Whiche to behold [whoo] were nat necligent,   313
   Receyved helth, salve, and medicyne
   Of al theyr hurtis, that were se*r*pentyne.   315

(46)

  This banner is most myghti of vertu,   316
   Geyns fiendes defence myghti and chief obstacle;

the sign of Tau shown to Ezekiel; the chief candelabrum of the tabernacle;
  Most noble signe and token of **Tau**
   To **Ezechiel** shewed by myracle;
  Chief chaundelabre of the tabernacle,   320

---

292 seen] se.   295 palme] pallis.   298 made] makid.
299 key] kepe.   302 ascencyon] Redempcioun H.   308 assaile] assaye.   309 poole] pale.   313 whoo] *om.* H.   318 **Tau**] chayne.

Wherthurgh was caused al his cliere light
Voidyng al derknesse of the clowdy nyght. 322

(47)
This was the tree of mankynde boote, 323   *the staff which sweetened the water of Marah;*
Thatt stynt hir wrath and brought in al the pees,
Whiche made the water of **Marath** fressh and swoote,
That was to-forne most bitter dout[e]les.
This was the yerd of worthy **Moyses**, 327   *the stick or Moses;*
Whiche made the children of Israel go free
And dry-footed thurgh the Rede See. 329

(48)
This was the slyng, [with] whiche with stones fyve   *the sling of David,*
Worthy **David**, as bookes specifie,
Gan the hede and the helme to-Rive
Of the Geaunt, that callid was **Golye**,
Whiche fyve stones, takyng the Allegorye, 334   *whose five stones signify Christ's five wounds.*
Arn the fyve woundes, as I reherse can,
With whiche that Crist venqwisshed **Sathan**.

(49)
O synful soule, why nyltow taken kepe 337   [leaf 234] *"O sinful soul,*
Of his peynes, Remembryng on the showres?
Forsake the world, and wake out of thy sleepe,   *forsake the world!*
And to the gardyn of perfite paramours
Make thy passage, and gadre there thy flowres 341
Of verray vertu, and chaunge al thyn old lyf,
And in that gardyn be contemplatyf! 343

(50)
*For this world here, both at Even and morwe, 344   *"It is but an exile.*
Who list considre aright in his Reasoun,
*Is but an exile and a desert of sorwe,
Meynt ay with trouble and tribulacioun;
But who list fynde consolacioun 348   *"If thou wilt find peace, come to the garden*
Of gostly Ioye, lete hym the worlde forsake
And to that gardyn the Right[e] wey[e] take, 350

---

321 -thurgh] -thorugh.   323 mankynde] mankyndes.
324 brought] bought.   329 thurgh] ouer.   330 1st with]
om. H A.   334 the Allegorye] palegorye.   336 venqwisshed]
venquysht hath.   344 For] From H.   346 Is] It is H.

II. Christ calls man's Soul as his Sister and Spouse.

(51)

mentioned in the Song of Songs.

Where-as [þat] god of love hym-self doth dwelle 351
Vpon an hille ferre from the mortal vale—
Canticorum the booke ful wele can telle—
Callyng his spouse with sugred notes smale,
Where that ful lowde the Amerous nyghtyngale 355
Vpon a thorn is wont to calle and crye
To mannes soule with hevenly Armonye: 357

(52)

'*Veni in ortum meum : soror mea.* 358

"Come thither to live in purity, as Christ's sister and bride:

Com to my gardyn and to myn herber grene,
My fayre suster and my spouse deere,
From filth of synne by vertu made al clene ;
With Cristal paved, thaleys bien so cliere. 362
Com, for I calle, anon and thow shalt heere.'
How Crist Ihesu, so blessid mote he be,
Callith mannes soule of perfite charite ! 365

(53)

He callith hir 'suster' and his 'spouse' also : 366
First his suster, who-so list to se,
As by nature—take goode heede herto !—

[leaf 234, bk.]

Ful nygh of kynne by consanguinite ;

Bride by affinity of grace,

And eke his spouse by affinyte,— 370
I meane as thus : be affynite of grace,—
With gostly love whan he doth it embrace ; 372

(54)

sister by nature, because Christ is the Virgin Mary's son, and our brother."

And eke his suster by semblaunce of nature, 373
Whan that he toke oure humanyte
Of a mayde most clennest and pure,
[. . . . . *no gap in the MS.*]
Fresshest of floures that sprang out of Iesse, 377
As flour ordeyned for to Releve man,
Whiche bare the fruyt that slough oure foo
Sathan." 379

Of this Balade Dan Iohñ
Lydgate made nomore.

351 þat] *om.* H. 353 **Canticorum**] -um *abbreviated;* canticoy A. 354 Callyng] called. 358 soror] sorar. 362 thaleys] paleys. 372 doth it] it doth. 379 bare] bore.

NOTES.

POEM I.

p. 1, line i. About this opening in prose compare *Introduction*, § 8.
l. iii. swañ] See *Gattinger*, p. 67.
l. v. With regard to the different ecclesiastical terms compare C. Horstmann, *Altenglische Legenden, Neue Folge;* Heilbronn, 1881, Introduction, and Emil Feiler, *Das Benediktiner-Offizium, ein altenglisches Brevier aus dem* 11. *Jahrhundert. Ein Beitrag zur Wulfstanfrage* (*Anglistische Forschungen* 4), Heidelberg, 1901, p. 11 ff.
'Horae,' hours, in the sense of the old Christian Church, means not only the hours of devotion, but the divine service itself, celebrated in these hours. Generally seven are mentioned—1. Nocturn, 2. Matins, 3. Prime, 4. Tierce, 5. Sexte, 6. Nones, 7. Vespers. As Prime was not observed everywhere, 8. Compline (completorium) was added in the 6th century, in order to get the full number of seven hours of divine service, as this number was considered to be commanded by the psalm cxviii, 164 : 'Septies in die laudem dixi tibi.'
l. vii. tercia] In the MS. there is a flourish attached to this word, similar to those which in Latin MSS. signify the termination of the gen. plur. -rum; see H. l. 353 : Canticorum. As this expansion would be mere nonsense here, I have omitted this sign altogether.
l. xv. Crucifige] occurs in the part which is dedicated to Tierce, l. 308.
p. 2, st. 1–4. The order of thoughts is as follows : The poet sends the little book to the Duchess, to present itself to her and to beseech her that she will take and keep it, till she gather her courtiers around her. These were always inclined to listen to the song of the "amerouse" nightingale, interpreting her song in a worldly way. Therefore the Duchess ought to read them the poet's song of the "gostly" nightingale, to drive their idle thoughts out of their hearts, which otherwise would be conquered again by the charms of the fresh month of May.
p. 2, l. 1. About "Go, lityll quayere . . ." see *Introduction*, § 6, and Schick, *T. G.* note to l. 1393.
dresse] instead of "adresse"; compare H. ll. 204, 226, 227, 229, 239, 265, 317, which I also do not consider as type E. This dropping of a first unaccented syllable often occurs in Lydgate. *M. P.* 12 ('rayed), 174, 175 ('mong); Schick, *T. G.* 875 (longip); Steele, *Secrees*, 526 (cordith); *Falls*, 143 b 2 (Gynneth); *Pilgr.* 1165 (cordyng). Compare also Skeat, *Chaucer*, iii, L. o. g. W. B. 359 (parteth=departeth) and v, Addenda, p. 493, note to l. A. 3287 (do wey, go wey = away).
l. 2. wyth humble reuerence] See *Æsop* (Zupitza) 271 :
The lambe answerd *with* humble reuerence.
l. 4. The Duches of Bokyngham] See § 2, A, 2, *Description of the MSS.*, and § 7, *The Date*.

p. 2, l. 4. of hur excellence] and l. 5 : of hure pacyence, and l. 6 : of hure noble grace—" of " denotes here the cause; compare Paul's *Grundriss der Germanischen Philologie*, ²i (Einenkel), p. 1104, § 155 λ).

M. P. 49 : Noble pryncessis of meek benyvolence,
Be example of hir your hornes cast away.

Rom. of the R. 3655, 3656 :
This is to sayne, that of his grace
He wolde me yeve leyser and space.

Ibid. 4604 : I praye Love, of his goodlihede.

S. of Thebes (Skeat) 1291 :
Beseching hire, only of her grace.

The same l. 142.

l. 5. of hure pacyence] See note to l. 4.
l. 6. of hure noble grace] See note to l. 4.
l. 8. Vnto the tyme] See Schick, *T. G.* note to l. 1082.
l. 9. Luste] The construction of this verb is very inconsistent in Lydgate; compare Schleich, *Fabula*, p. lxv; Degenhart, *Hors*, note to l. 127. In our poems compare also, e. g. : c. ll. 174, 175 ; H., ll. 50, 110, 111, 237, 345, 348 ; both constructions in one sentence we find *Falls*, 40 a 2 :

But such as list not corrected be,
by example of other fro vicious gouernaunce
and fro their vices list not for to flee.

l. 11. primetens] Compare l. 23. *Pilgr.* 3455 :
At prymë temps, with many a flour.

Rom. of the R. 3373 :
At primë temps, Love to manace.

Ibid. 4534 : At prymë temps of his foly.

But *ibid.* 4747 :
Prymę temps, ful of frostes whyte.

l. 16. gostly sense] There are among the *M. P.* (*Minor Poems*, Percy Soc.) some verses, entitled " Make amendes," where likewise the song of a little bird is interpreted "in gostly sense," but the poem is not considered to be Lydgatian (compare *Gattinger*, p. 78). I cite here the first two stanzas (p. 228 f.):

By a wylde wodes syde	" Make amende trewely ; "
As I walked myself alone,	Than song that bryd with federes gray,
A blysse of bryddes me bad abyde,	In myne hert fulle woo was y,
For cause there song mo then one ;	Whan "make amendes" he gan to say ;
Among thes bryddes everych one,	I stode and studyede alle that day,
Full gret hede y gan take,	Thes word made me alle nygth to wake,
How he gon syng with rewfully mone,	Than fond I by good schyle, in fay,
" Mon, y rede the, amendes make."	Why he sede " amendes make."

For a worldly song of a nightingale compare, e. g. *Kingis Quair*, st. 34.

l. 19. But] refers to "bare of eloquence."
l. 20. vnlawfle] Lydgate probably read "vnlawful"; in this way the hiatus is also avoided ; see l. 65.
l. 22. vertu] See note to H., l. 316.
l. 25. freshe May] Schick, *T. G.* 184 :
For it ne sit not vnto fressh[e] May.

l. 26. Phebus and Titan (compare l. 92 and H., l. 1) are very common for the sun, see Schick, *T. G.* note to ll. 4–7, and the following quotations :

Schick, *T. G.* 272 :
    Lich Phebus bemys shynyng in his spere.
Edmund, i, 314 :
    Shyne in vertu as Phebus in his speer.
Voss. Gg. 9, f. 76 b :
    Which be nyght as Phebus in his spire.
M. P. 182 :   Til on a morwe, whan Tytan shone ful clere,
Ibid. 195 :   Titan to erly whan he his cours doth dresse.
Ibid. 216 :   So as Phebus perceth thoruhe the glas
    With brihte beemys, shynyng in his speere.
Falls, 3 a 1 : highe as Phebus shineth in his sphere.
Skeat, *Chaucer*, vii, x, 114 :
    O fyry Tytan, persing with thy bemes.
Schleich, *Fabula*, 688 :
    And nyht approchith, whan Titan is gon doun.
Skeat, *Chaucer*, vii, ix, 265-266 :
    The foules alle, whan Tytan did springe,
    With devout herte, me thoughte I herde singe!

p. 3, l. 29-32. A similar passage occurs in Skeat, *Chaucer*, i, 3, 16-27 :

And wel ye wite, agaynes kinde   And I ne may, ne night ne morwe,
Hit were to liven in this wyse ;   Slepe ; and thus melancolye,
For nature wolde nat suffyse   And dreed I have for to dye,
To noon erthely creature   Defaute of slepe, and hevinesse
Not longe tyme to endure   Hath sleyn my spirit of quiknesse,
Withoute slepe, and been in sorwe ; That I have lost al lustihede.

l. 29. nedes most] Compare C. Stoffel in *Englische Studien* 28 (1900), p. 303 ff. See also ll. 157, 181.

l. 33. kyndely] See Degenhart, *Hors*, note to l. 512, Mätzner, and note l. 294 of our poem.

ll. 34, 35. It is a very common idea to represent the nightingale as singing all the night. Compare l. 100 of our poem and the following quotations : *M. P.* 153 :
    Nyhtynggales al nyght syngen and wake,
    For long absence and wantyng of his make.
Skeat, *Chaucer*, iv, *C. T.*, A. 98 :
    He sleep namore than dooth a nightingale.
Ibid. vii, xxiv, 1355-6 :
    He (*i. e.* the nightingale) might not slepe in all the nightertale,
    But '*Domine labia*,' gan he crye and gale.
Percy Society, vii : *The Harmony of Birds*, ed. by J. Payne Collier, p. 6 :
    Than sayd the nightyngale,
    To make shorte tale,
      For wordes I do refuse,
    Because my delyght,
    Both day and nyght
      Is synging for to use.
Ibid. xi : *The Owl and the Nightingale*, ed. by Thomas Wright, p. 16 :
    Bit me that ich shulle singe
    Vor hire luve one skentinge ;
    And ich [*i. e.* the nightingale] so do thurȝ niȝt and dai.
Ibid. p. 26 :   Ich singe mid hom niȝt and dai.

Confessio Amantis (E. E. T. S., E. S. 81), p. 378, ll. 2872–2874:
>I thenke upon the nyhtingale,
>Which slepeth noght be weie of kinde
>For love, in bokes as I finde.

Ibid. (E. E. T. S., E. S. 82), p. 109, l. 5976:
>Wher as sche [*i. e.* Philomene] singeth day and nyht.

George Gascoigne in *Specimens of the Early English Poets*, London 1790, p. 23:
>And as fair *Philomene* again
>Can watch and sing when others sleep,
>And taketh pleasure in her pain,
>To wray the woe that makes her weep.

p. 3, l. 35. set no tale] Compare G. L. Kittredge, *Authorship of the Romaunt of the Rose (Studies and Notes in Philology and Literature,* i), Boston, 1892, p. 39. I add the following quotations out of works of Lydgate:

Degenhart, *Hors*, 440:
>Sette litil store of swerde or arwis kene.

Ibid. 479: Whiche, of madness, bi wolle set no fors.

Ibid. 237 (and note to this line):
>And, for he set of me that day no fors.

Pilgr. 4718, 4719:
>And I am she that set no cure
>Off grucchyng nor detraccïoun.

Falls, 199 a 2: Fortune of me set now but litle prise.
Ibid. 210 b 2: Of his manace set but litle tale.

Æsop (Sauerstein), iv. 116:
>To ouerpresse a pore man the riche set no tale.

Also, *Confessio Amantis* (E. E. T. S., E. S. 81), p. 53, ll. 649, 650:
>. . . . . for of the smale
>As for tacompte he set no tale.

Ibid. p. 330, ll. 1062, 1063:
>And of the conseil non accompte
>He sette, ...

Ibid. p. 347, l. 1716:
>For al ne sette I at a stre.

Ibid. (E. E. T. S., E. S. 82), p. 197, ll. 1130, 1131:
>Withinne his herte he set no pris
>Of al the world, ...

Ibid. p. 329, l. 3342:
>Which mannes lif sette of no pris.

l. 37. The same sequence of rhymes as in ll. 37, 39, and 40 occurs also in Skeat, *Chaucer*, iv, *C. T.*, B. 1735-7-8, and *ibid.* vii, xviii, 71-2-5: rote-note-throte.

l. 38. dry or wete, derk or lyght] It is not altogether unusual with Lydgate that the thesis is wanting in enumeration; compare Degenhart, *Hors*, p. 37. Perhaps we are allowed to assume the same metrical phenomenon in l. 397 of our poem, and in *Falls*, 82 b 2:
>Breake his coller thicke, double, and longe.

l. 39. be rote] About the etymology of this word consult *Stratmann-Bradley*, article 'route,' Skeat, *Chaucer*, vi, p. 218; vii, p. 527, and

Notes: Poem I. Page 3, lines 41-57.

Confessio Amantis (E. E. T. S., E. S. 82), p. 515, note to l. 1312. It occurs also in *M. P.* 152 :
   Suych labourerys synge may be roote.
and Skeat, *Chaucer*, iv, *C. T.*, B. 1735 :
   Fro day to day, til he coude it by rote.
Ibid. vii, xviii, 71 :
   They coude that servyce al by rote.
   p. 3, l. 41. Lydgate is very fond of the construction exhibited by this line.
M. P. 4 :   That to behold it whas a noble sighte.
Ibid. 181 :   That to beholde it was an hevenly sighte.
G. W. (Robinson), 360 :
   That to be-holde hit was verray wondre.
Falls, 81 b 2 : That to beholde it was an ougly syght.
S. of Thebes, 376 b 1 :
   That to beholde, it was a verie wonder.
Similarly in *Kingis Quair*, st. 162, l. 3 :
   That to behald thereon I quoke for fere.
Compare also : *Court of Sapience*, f. 1 b :
   That heuen it was to here her beauperlaunce.
Skeat, *Chaucer*, iv, *C. T.*, F. 271 :
   That it is lyk an heven for to here.
   ll. 43-45. Compare for the explanation of these lines, Schick, *T. G.* p. cxiv, and note 1, and also Skeat, *Chaucer*, ii, p. 468.
   l. 46. 'Whech' and 'hir'] refer to 'May,' l. 45. The poet probably had in mind the idea of an allegoric personification or a goddess of May.
   l. 46. thoo] refers to 'sleep' and 'bed,' l. 44. The sense is : Overmuch sleep is not in harmony with the merry month of May : poets, lovers, etc., go forth early at that season
   'To do obeissance to the month of May.'
   l. 47. thoght] means 'heavy thought, trouble.' See Schick, *T. G.* l. 1 and note. Also in *Hoccleve* (E. E. T. S., E. S. 72), p. 10, ll. 239, 240 :
   I haue herd seyn, in kepyng of richesse
   Is thoght and wo, & besy a-wayte al-way.
Ibid. l. 245 :   þus poght turmentiþ folk in sondry kynde.
Ibid. p. 11, l. 267 :
   Be war of þoght, for it is perillous.
   l. 51. As fer as] see Schick, *T. G.* note to l. 1029.
   l. 52. So] without continuation in the following part of the sentence.
   l. 54. daye-rowes] See *Introduction*, § 5, Schick, *T. G.* p. lxix, and Kraussner, *Complaint*, p. 25.
   l. 54. can] =gan =began, without any proper meaning; compare, *e.g.* ll. 136, 339, 395, and H., li. 19, 144, (156, 158, 332); also Ellis, *E. E. P.* i, p. 375, and Degenhart, *Hors*, l. 137 and note.
   l. 55. Ymagynyng—56. calde] Perhaps it would have been preferable to enclose this parenthesis within dashes.
   l. 57. Lydgate likes to join these alliterative words. *Falls*, 173 a 1 :
   Of superfluitie, of slouth and of slepe.
Kk. i. f. 194 b :
   That slombre & sleepe // þe longe wynteres nygt.
Æsop (Sauerstein), ii, 77 :
   And suche folke to rebuken, that levyn in slombir and slowth.
M. P. 68 :   And slowth at morow, and slomberyng idelnes.
NIGHTINGALE.   D

Ibid. 236 :   Fro slouthe and slombre mysilf I shal restreyne.
Venus-Mass, MS. Fairfax, f. 314 b :
      In slep / slogardye / and slouthe.
(quoted from E. E. T. S. 71).
Also Skeat, *Chaucer*, vii, xxiv, 649 :
      Trowbled I was with slomber, slepe, and slouth.
And *Hoccleve* (E. E. T. S., E. S. 72), p. xxvi, l. 93 :
      Puttyng awey thi slombre & [thi] slouthe.

p. 4, l. 63. laurer grene] The nightingale represented as sitting on a laurel occurs also in Skeat, *Chaucer*, vii, xx, 109 :
      Wher she (*i. e.* the nightingale) sat in a fresh green laurer-tree.
Ibid. 435, 436 :
      For then the nightingale, that al the day
      Had in the laurer sete, ...
   The laurel has very often the epitheton 'green': *Flour of Curtesye*, f. 248 a 2 :
      I set me downe, vnder a laurer grene.
Ibid. f. 249 a 2 :
      Fayrest in our tonge, as the Laurer grene.
   Also Skeat, *Chaucer*, vii, xx, 268 and 289, and Krausser, *Complaint*, 65. In the *Canterbury Tales* Chaucer tells us why the laurel got this epithet : Skeat, *Chaucer*, iv, C. T., E. 1465, 1466 :
      Myn herte and alle my limes been as grene
      As laurer thurgh the yeer is for to sene.
And Lydgate himself states, *M. P.* 180 :
      And the laurealle of nature is ay grene.
   Compare also the following lines from *Confessio Amantis* (E. E. T. S., E. S. 81), p. 272, ll. 1716–1720 :
      This Daphne into a lorer tre
      Was torned, which is evere grene,
      In tokne, as yit it mai be sene,
      That sche schal duelle a maiden stille,
      And Phebus failen of his wille.

l. 65. wilfle] See note to l. 20.
l. 70. Compare l. 179.
l. 71. morowe gray] This motif reminds us of the beginning of the 'Flour of Curtesye,' where we hear that the lark sings (*Flour of Curtesye*, 248 a 1) :
      Ful lustely, againe the morowe gray.
M. P. 23 :   And Aurora, ageyne the morowe gray.
   It occurs also among the poems of Charles d'Orléans, iii (Wülcker, *Altenglisches Lesebuch*, ii.), p. 123, 2 :
      Aftir the sterry nyght the morow gray.
But *ibid., Story of Thebes*, 9 :
      When Aurora was in the morowe redde.
Compare also Skeat, *Chaucer*, i, 4, 1 :
      Gladeth, ye foules, of the morow gray.
Ibid. iv, C. T., A. 1491, 1492 :
      The bisy larke, messager of day,
      Saluëth in hir song the morwe gray.

l. 74. For] = in spite of ; compare Paul's *Grundriss*, i, 1102 *ι*, and *e. g.* :
M. P. 215 :   Blenchithe never for al the cliere light.

Skeat, *Chaucer*, iv, *C. T.*, C. 129 :
   This mayde shal be myn, for any man.
Ibid. i, 3, 534, 535 :
   Right wonder skilful and resonable,
   As me thoghte, for al his bale.
See also l. 273.
   p. 4, l. 78. Contynving] Lydgate uses normally the other form of this verb : 'contune'; compare Brotanek, *Die Englischen Maskenspiele*, p. 309, ll. 3, 4 : ffortune—contune rhyming with each other; Schick, *T. G.* 'contuned' 390 rhyming with 'vnfortuned' 389 ; 'contune' 1333 rhyming with 'fortune' 1332.
   l. 82. thorg-oute the wode yt ronge] Compare Krausser, *Complaint*, 44, 45:
   Which (*i. e.* the briddes) on the braunches, bothe in pleyn [and] vale,
   So loude songe that al the wode ronge.
   To the quotations given in the note to l. 45 add the following ones from Skeat, *Chaucer*, vii, xx, 99, 100 :
      The nightingale with so mery a note
      Answered him, that al the wodë rong.
Ibid. vii, xviii, 96-100 :
      And as I with the cukkow thus gan chyde,
      I herde, in the nexte bush besyde,
      A Nightingalë so lustily singe
      That with her clere vois she made ringe
      Through-out al the grene wode wyde.
   Thomas Wright, *Specimens of Lyric Poetry*, Percy Society, iv (1841), p. 43 :
      This foules singeth ferly fele,
      Ant wlyteth on huere wynter wele,
      that al the wode ryngeth.
   ll. 88, 89. These two lines may be a reminiscence from the Latin original, ii, 3-4 :
      Tollens eius taedia vice dulcis lyrae,
      Quem, heu ! modo nequeo verbis convenire.
   p. 5, l. 90. euer among] Compare note to H., l. 61.
   Ocy] = the call of the nightingale, occurs in our poems here and l. 98, in H., ll. 14, 55, 59, 85, 217. Compare *Uhlands Schriften zur Geschichte der Dichtung und Sage*, iii, Stuttgart, 1866, p. 97 f. ; Reinhold Köhler, *Kleinere Schriften*. Hrsg. von Joh. Bolte, Berlin, 1900, iii, No. 32, pp. 216-218 (also in : *Zeitschrift für romanische Philologie*, viii (1884), pp. 120-122) ; Gustav Thurau, *Der Refrain in der französischen Chanson*, Berlin, 1901 [*Litterarhistorische Forschungen*, hrsg. von J. Schick und M. v. Waldberg, No. 23], p. 73 ff.
   In mediæval literature we meet not unfrequently with this imitation of the nightingale's song. The quotations which have come to my knowledge may be divided into two main groups : The poets of the one use 'ocy' as an onomatopœia for her plaintive song, those of the other interpret it as an imperative, addressed by the bird to the hearer.
   To the first group belong the author of Lydgate's Latin original, Peckham (?), and the greater number of his imitators (see also *Introduction*, p. xxxix, note 5), as *e. g.* Jacobus de Porta, Diepenbrock, Anonymus S. (*Des hl. Bonaventura Philomele oder Nachtigallenlied*, Lingen, 1883), and C. Fortlage (*Gesänge christlicher Vorzeit*, Berlin, 1844). There are with the latter but slight varieties in reproducing 'oci' : J. de Porta by

'ochij,' Diepenbrock by 'oci,' Anonymus S. and Fortlage by 'ozi.' Only Jacobus Balde (*Poematum tomus* iv, *Coloniae Ubiorum*, 1660) attempts an allegoric interpretation :

Pars. iv. :   . . . cum sol medium flagrantior igne scandit axem
Illâ, nescio quos, crebro vocat impotenter hora.
Ocyus, exclamans, huc *ocyus, ocyus* venite.
Ocyus, advolita soror *ocyus, ocyus,* sorori.
Adriacum rapidis toties mare non tumet procellis
Nec folia arboribus, simul ingruit Africus, moventur :
Multa suum quoties canit ocyus, ocyusque plorat.

Pars. xxi. : *Oti* blanda quies, dulcedo nobilis *oti*,
Recepta Cordis angulo
Mens **Philomela** canit.

The other group is represented chiefly by French poets, many of whom understand 'oci' as the imperative mood of 'occir' = kill, and use it both in epic and lyric poetry, e. g. :

Histoire littéraire de la France, xxii, p. 345 (also in Martonne, *Analyse du roman de dame Aye*, p. 23) :

Et chantent li oisel et mainent grant delit,
Et li roussignolet qui dit : Oci, oci !
Pucelle est en effroi qui loing set son ami.

Guillaume le Vinier in *Histoire littéraire*, xxiii, p. 592 f. :

Trop a mon cuer esjoï
Li louseignols qu'ai oï,
Qui chantant dist :
Fier fier, oci oci,
Ceux par cui sont esbaï
Fin amant.

Wistasse le Moine, hrsg. von Wendelin Foerster und Johann Trost, Halle, 1891 [*Romanische Bibliothek*, hrsg. von W. Foerster, 4], ll. 1142 ff. :

Illuecques se fist loussignol.   "Ochi ! ochi ! ochi ! ochi ! "
Bien tenoit le conte por fol.   Et li quens Renaus respondi :
Quant voit le conte trespasser,   "Je l'ocirai, par saint Richier !
Wistasces commenche a criër :   Se je le puis as mains ballier."

Compare W. W. Comfort in *Modern Language Notes*, xiii (1898), col. 513 ff.

Charles de Bourdigné, Faitz & Dictz Joyeulx de Pierre Faifeu, Paris, 1833 [*Trésor des vieux poëtes français*, 6], pp. 23, 24 :

Me pourmenant, ung Roussignol s'esveille ;
De son doulx chant très fort je me esmerveille,
Quar il disoit en son chant : " Fy, fy, fy,
Fy de dormir, fy d'homme qui sommeille,
Fy de songeard, fy d'homme qui ne veille
A son honneur." Alors je vous affy
Que j'heu bien peur & ung très grant deffy
De perdre honneur par ma grant nonchallance,
Veu qu'on ne acquiert sans bien grant[s] porchatz lance.

Je l'escoutté ; lors commença à dire,
Tournant son chant mieulx que une harpe ou lire,
En chaht bien doulx & plaisant : "Suy, suy, suy."
A l'escouter je ne peuz contredire,
Mais suis faché, quasi rencontré de ire,
Que ne le voy, & il semble estre icy,
Car il disoit : " Vien tost, aussy, aussy ;

Notes: Poem I. Page 5, line 90.

> Ne sois lassé ; le gaing est à poursuyvre " :
> Tel va bien tost qu'on aconsuyt pour suyvre.

Compare *Wistasse*, ed. Foerster, note to l. 1146.
Huon de Méry, Li tornoiemenz Antecrit. Hrsg. von Georg Wimmer, Marburg, 1888 [*Ausgaben und Abhandlungen.* Hrsg. von E. Stengel, 76], ll. 3295–3298 :

> Et li rousignous ça *et* ci
> Crie : 'Fui ! Fui !—Oci ! Oci !'
> Si que sa menace tormente
> Tout le vergier.

Raynaud, *Recueil de Motets français* (Bibl. fr. du m.-âge), Paris, 1881, i, p. 49 :

> Et si orrons le roussignol chanter
> En l'ausnoi,
> Qui dit : *Oci ceus qui n'ont le cuer gai,*
> *Douce Marot, grief sont li mau d'amer.*

Skeat, *Chaucer*, vii : The Cuckoo and the Nightingale, ll. 121–135 :

> And every wight may understande me ;
> But, Nightingale, so may they not do thee ;
> For thou hast many a nyce queinte cry.
> I have herd thee seyn, "*ocy! ocy!*"
> How mighte I knowe what that shulde be ? '
> ' A fole ! ' quod she, ' wost thou not what it is ?
> Whan that I say "*ocy! ocy!*" y-wis,
> Than mene I that I wolde, wonder fayn,
> That alle they were shamfully y-slayn
> That menen aught ayeines love amis.
> And also I wolde alle tho were dede
> That thenke not in love hir lyf to lede ;
> For who that wol the god of love not serve,
> I dar wel say, is worthy for to sterve ;
> And for that skil "*ocy! ocy!*" I grede.'

To these we may also reckon the quotations from the poetry of the troubadours alluded to by *Thurau*, p. 75.

Though 'ocy' does not verbally occur, we must necessarily suppose the same idea in *Jourdains de Blaivies* in *Amis et Amiles und Jourdains de Blaivies.* Hrsg. von C. Hofmann, Erlangen, 1882, ll. 1546–1550 :

> En un vergier s'en entra maintenant,
> Dou rousseingnol i a oi le chant,
> Cil autre oisel se vont esbanoiant.
> Lors li ramembre de Fromont le tyrant,
> Qu'ocist son pere a l'espee tranchant . . .

In some cases I am not able to classify the quotations, *e. g. Uhland,* p. 167, 198, from a manuscript in Strassburg, fol. 37 a :

> He tres dous rousignol ioli
> qui dis oci oci oci, etc.

Or Godefroy, *Dictionnaire de l'ancienne langue française*, Paris, 1881–95, from R. de Houdenc, Meraugis, MS. Vienne, f. 28 c :

> Quant j'oi chanter a mes oreilles
> Le roussignol *oci, oci*.

Later instances prove that this second group has degenerated and that the idea of 'ocy' as an imperative has been effaced by degrees, so

38 *Notes: Poem I. Page 5, lines 92–108.*

that the two groups again coincide at last. Compare *La Curne de Sainte-Palaye, Dictionnaire historique de l'ancien langage françois*, Niort—Paris [1880, viii] :

J'oie oi le roxignol mener,   Oci, oci, vilaine gent :
Qui me fet plaindre, et dolouser,   Jolis cuer doit bien amer,
Por les maus que je sens por li,   Par amours joliement.
Qui sor l'arbre chante à haut cri,   (MS. 7218, f. 271.)

Pourquoi tient on le chant à gracieus
D'un ozeillon qu'on claimme rossegnol ?
Pour ce qu'il est jolis, et amoureus, . . .
Et dist *occi, occi*, joieus, joieus.   (Froiss. Poës. p. 336.)

Le rossignol crie, sur les ramssiaux,
Vray messaige d'amour entretenir,
Occy, occy, entre vous damoisiaux . . .   (Desch. f. 164.)

See also *Thurau*, p. 74.

Finally, how have we to classify the lines in our poems ? To the first group we have to reckon H., ll. 55, 59, 85, 217, whereas to the second evidently belongs H., l. 14, as it is proved by ll. 20, 106. The two lines from c., however, ll. 90, 98, exhibit another trace of Lydgate's originality, in so far as these are the only lines where 'ocy' refers to the death of the nightingale herself.

Compare also Arnold Pischinger, *Der Vogelgesang bei den griechischen Dichtern des klassischen Altertums. Ein Beitrag zur Würdigung des Naturgefühls der antiken Poesie. Programm des K. humanistischen Gymnasiums Eichstätt für das Schuljahr* 1900/01, Eichstätt, 1901.

p. 5, l. 92. Phebus] See note to l. 26.
l. 93. Ouer] to be read as a monosyllable.
ll. 94, 95. *M. P.* 24 :

The golden chayre of Phebus in the eyre
Chasith mistis blake, ...

l. 98. Ocy] See note l. 90.
l. 100. Compare note to ll. 34, 35.
l. 103. she] 'Hir' l. 104, and 'she' l. 105 wrongly refer to 'bryd' l. 101. The poet certainly was thinking of 'nightingale' instead of 'bird.' Compare ll. 106, 107, and H. ll. 56, 72, 73.

l. 105. I may be allowed to insert here two quotations from Grimm, J. und W., *Deutsches Wörterbuch*, vii, Leipzig, 1889 :

mir geschihet von ir minne sunder wanc
als der nahtegal, diu sitzet tôt ob ir vröuden sanc.
minnesinger 1, 28b Hagen.

Megenberg : diu nahtigal . . . singt gar ämsicleich und gar frävenlich über ir kraft alsô groezleich, daz si sô krank wirt, daz si sterben muoz.— 221, 4 ff. (vergl. Plinius 10, 83 : certant inter se, palamque animosa contentio est. victa morte finit saepe vitam spiritu prius deficiente quam cantu).

ll. 106, 107. About 'brid'—'her' see note to l. 103. 'brid,' with poetical licence, is put instead of 'the story of this bird.'

l. 108. latyn—boke] See *Introduction*, § 8, and *Gattinger*, p. 73.
versed] Compare *uersie* = versify in Skeat, *Piers Plowman*, C. 18, 108–10 :

For þer is nouthe non · who so nymeþ hede,
That can [versifie][1] fayre · oþer formeliche endite,
Ne þat can construen kyndeliche · þat poetes maden.

[1] uersie, P.

Notes: Poem I. Pages 5, 6, lines 114–137. 39

p. 5, l. 114. I was not able to find out any passage in the Holy Scripture to which Lydgate alludes here.

ll. 115, 116. cristen-man Soule] Perhaps we have here an example of a genitive case without ending? Compare Gough, *On the Middle English Metrical Romance of Emare*, p. 7, and also the following quotations:
Percy Soc. xiv: *Poems of John Audelay*, ed. by J. O. Halliwell,
 p. 26: Fore mon soule thai schuld save.
 p. 27: To save mon soule spesialy.
 p. 36: Mon soul with mekenes to have in kepyng.
 p. 46: Serrs, so is mons soule with the sacrement.
 p. 47: That han the cure of mons soule in ȝoure kepyng.
 p. 48: And manse soule that was forjuggyd to damnacioun.
Again, *Hoccleve* (E. E. T. S., E. S. 72), p. 175, l. 4862:
 ffor a kyng is but a man soul, parfay!

ll. 116, (117). oweth] with infinitive without 'to,' see Mätzner, *Englische Grammatik*,³ Berlin, 1885, iii, p. 6.

p. 6, l. 120 ff. Compare *William of Shoreham*, ed. by Wright (Percy Society, xxviii), pp. 82–89.

l. 126. Compare Schick, *T. G.*, note to l. 761, Triggs, *Assembly*, Introduction, p. lxxii f., and Morrill, *Speculum*, notes to ll. 109 and 638.

ll. 129, 130. This idea may be suggested from the allegoric struggle in the Psychomachia by Prudentius, or by Ephes. vi, 10–17. Compare Schleich, *Fabula*, 595:
 Than the to arme strongly in pacience.
M. P. 177: I fond a lyknesse depict upon a wal,
 Armed in vertues, as I walk up and doun.
Ayenbite, ed. by R. Morris, p. 203:
. . . þet ofte recordeþ þane dyaþ and þe pine of Iesu crist. Vor þet is þe armure þet þe dyeuel dret mest . . .
Hoccleve (E. E. T. S., E. S. 72), p. 194, l. 5376:
 With pees and restë, armë yow and clothe!
Yorkshire Writers, Rolle of Hampole, ii, p. 112, l. 5, f. a:
 and arme hym with that holy passyon.
See also H., l. 285.

l. 130. quert] On this word, compare J. O. Halliwell, *Dictionary of Archaisms and Provincialisms*, London, 1846-7; Herbert Coleridge, *A Dictionary of the Oldest Words in the English Language*, London, 1862; *New English Dictionary*; *Sir Gowther*, ed. Breul, Oppeln, 1886, note to ll. 223, 224, and *Lay Folks' Mass-Book* (E. E. T. S. 71), p. 341, note to ll. 26, 27. It is very often found in *Rolle de Hampole's* writings, especially in his translation of the Psalms. Again it occurs in the *Catholicon Anglicanum* (E. E. T. S. 75), pp. 196 and 296, and *Political, Religious, and Love Poems* (E. E. T. S. 15), pp. 166/114, 167/111, 174/236, 175/103. Also *Hoccleve* knows it as an adjective (E. E. T. S., E. S. 72), p. 39, l. 1061:
 Nay! be þou riche or poore, or seke or quert.
Besides, in Lydgate, *M. P.*, where also the adjective occurs:
 p. 32: But she have al than, thouhe he be nat querte.
 p. 38: As Sampson did, whil he was hole and quert.

l. 136. can] See note to l. 54.

l. 137. mischeue] The following three quotations are taken from the *Century Dictionary* and *Stratmann-Bradley:*
 When pryde is moste in prys,

Ande couetyse moste wys, ...
Thenne schall Englonde mys-chewe.
Booke of Precedence (E. E. T. S., E. S), i, 85.

Merueile it is þat y not myscheeue,
þat y neere kild, drowned, or brent.
E. E. T. S. 15, p. 195, ll. 431, 432.

.... and up thai wol atte eve
Into a tree lest thai by nyght myscheve.
E. E. T. S. 52, i, 613, 614.

In the *Manipulus Vocabulorum* (E. E. T. S. 27), I found, col. 53, l. 14: to Mischéefe, *destruère*.

p. 6, l. 141. Before whos deth] The relative instead of the demonstrative pronoun, in order to effect a closer connection with the preceding sentence (compare Paul's *Grundriss*, i, p. 1119, ɛ, and Spies, *Studien zur Geschichte des Englischen Pronomens im XV. und XVI. Jahrhundert*, Halle, 1897, p. 222, § 230 ff.). See also l. 343.

l. 142. of] See note to l. 4.

offens, cleped originall] In Forcellini, *Totius Latinitatis Lexicon*, Prati, 1858, we find under the heading 'originalis' (2) the following remark: 'Speciatim apud Scriptores Ecclesiasticos *originale peccatum* dicitur illud priorum parentum in posteros generatione transfusum. *Augustin* 1. *de Anim.* 9. *n.* 10. et alibi.' This quotation from St. Augustine runs as follows: Sed utcumque sentiens quid mali dixerit, sine ulla Christi gratia animas redimi parvulorum in æternam vitam regnumque cœlorum, et in eis posse solvi originale peccatum sine Baptismo Christi, in quo fit remissio peccatorum: videns ergo, in quam se profunditatem naufragosi gurgitis jecerit, "Sane," inquit ....

11. Hoc enim eis etiam haeresis Pelagiana promisit: quia nec damnationem metuit parvulis, quos nullum putat habere originale peccatum ....

Lydgate, being a cleric himself, of course often makes use of this theological term. It occurs in the form 'synne orygynal,' *Pilgr.* 986, 1139 ff., 1158, 1255, 1280, also as 'orygynal trespace,' *ibid.* 1276. Again I noticed it in Skeat, *Chaucer*, vii, iv, 348, and *ibid.* iv, *C. T.* I, 334 and 808. Percy Soc. 28: *Poems of William de Shoreham*, ed. by T. Wright, p. 105:

Oryginale thys senne hys cleped,
For man of kende hyt taketh syn.

Hoccleve (E. E. T. S., E. S. 61), p. 46, l. 85:

þat for our gilt original wern slayn.

Confessio Amantis (E. E. T. S., E. S. 81, 82), v, 1767; vi, 1.

l. 143. infecte] = infected, as 'depeint' = depeinted (compare Schick, *T. G.*, note to l. 44; Hoccleve, E. E. T. S., E. S. 72, l. 5003), or 'depict' = depicted (*M. P.* 177, 259), and 'detecte' = detected (Percy Society, xi, ii: *Thirteen Psalms*, p. 10). Mätzner, however, in the dictionary to his *Altenglische Sprachproben*, article 'infecten,' doubts whether it is contracted from 'infected' or not, but considers it rather a form directly taken from the Latin. Quotations of this verb are also given in Schleich, *Fabula*, p. 104, to which we add the following ones:

Steele, *Secrees*, 1272:

Of enfect placys / Causyng the violence.

Pilgr. 5792:

Swych as be nat infect with synne.

Skeat, *Chaucer*, vii, xxiv, 217:

And punish me, with trespace thus enfect.

Notes: Poem I. Page 7, *lines* 150–168. 41

But *ibid.* vii, xxiv, 1053:
  Her gentilness may not infected be.
Hoccleve (E. E. T. S., E. S. 72), p. 171, ll. 4742, 4743:
  And a-mong othir þingës, þat your wilne
  Be infecte wiþ no wrecched chyncherie.
Hoccleve (E. E. T. S., E. S. 61), p. 117, l. 194:
  that so myche of this land / shall be infecte
(rhyming with: correcte (inf.) and secte).
  p. 7, l. 150. paradise] The metre requires if not elision of, then certainly slurring over the second syllable: par'dise.
M. P. 209: The stoon of paradys was fyn of his labour.
Ibid. 235: Man to restoore to paradys, his cité.
Albon and Amphabel (Horstmann), 1, 261:
  It was a paradise vpon hem to se.
Steele, *Secrees*, 627:
  It was a paradys / verray incomparable.
Kk. i, f. 195 b:
  The theeff / of Paradyse / made a sitesiene.
R. of the Rose, 648:
  Have been in paradys erth[e]ly.
  l. 151. sely] has here rather the meaning of 'unfortunate, fatal' as *e. g.* Schleich, *Fabula*, 589, 590:
  O seely marchaunt, myn hand I feele quake
  To write thy woo in my translacioun.
Skeat, *Chaucer*, iii, p. 162, l. 2339:
  O sely Philomene! wo is thyn herte.
  l. 156. *Holland's Buke of the Houlate*, ed. by A. Diebler, l. 976:
  Think how bair thow wes borne, and bair ay will be.
  l. 157. nedes mvst] Compare note to l. 29.
  ll. 160, 161. A similar thought is met with in *Ayenbite of Inwyt*, ed. by R. Morris, p. 71:
  Vor huanne þou begonne libbe: anhaste þou begonne to sterue.
Yorkshire Writers, Rolle of Hampole, ii, p. 36, ll. 21–24:
  For fro bigynnyng of oure childehede
  ilk day to dye we are dredande;
  þen þis [lif] is faylande at þo nede,
  for whils we here lyue [we] are dyande.
Also in *Anglia*, vii (1884), *Anzeiger*, p. 85, ll. 17, 18:
  For yn þe oure of oure natyvyte
  Thy [*i. e.* death] sotell entre us perschet everychon.
Nearly the same idea occurs again, Skeat, *Chaucer*, iv, *C. T.*, A. 3891 ff.:
  For sikerly, whan I was bore, anon
  Deeth drogh the tappe of lyf and leet it gon;
  And ever sith hath so the tappe y-ronne,
  Til that almost al empty is the tonne.
I could not find out where this idea is borrowed from.
  ll. 164–168. A similar passage occurs in Morrill, *Speculum* (E. E. T. S., E. S. 75), ll. 215–222:

And ȝaf to man fre power   Wheiþer he wole chese, he haþ power
To chese, boþe fer and ner,   þurw ȝifte of god, while he is her;
Off god and yuel shed to make, þanne is hit noht on god ilong,
þe euel to late *and* god to take. If man wole chese to don wrong,

The note to l. 215, p. 66, rightly points out the different opinion of Chaucer on this subject, referring to Skeat, *Chaucer*, *C. T.*, B., ll. 4424-4441; especially ll. 4433-4438:

>Whether that goddes worthy forwiting
>Streyneth me nedely for to doon a thing,
>(Nedely clepe I simple necessitee);
>Or elles, if free choys be graunted me
>To do that same thing, or do it noght,
>Though god forwoot it, er that it was wroght.

The following quotations, however, will prove, as it seems to me, that Lydgate's dogmatic point of view was more generally adopted. I noticed similar passages in *Yorkshire Writers, Rolle of Hampole*, ii, p. 45, ll. 753, 754:

>And þerfore chese þe, or þou wende,
>wheþer þou wolt to payne or blis.

Percy Society, xiv, 1: *Poems of John Audelay*, ed. by J. O. Halliwell, p. 8:

>Better mon ys made resnabyl,
>Good and evyl to have in his mynd;
>And has fre choys, as we fynde,
>Weder he wyl do good or ylle,
>Owther y-savyd or ellys y-schent,
>Owther have heven or ellus have hell,
>   thou hast fre choys.

Ibid. p. 52:

>For thou ast fre choyse to ryse or falle,
>   Both thou may.

Ibid. p. 53:

>Here twey wayes [*i. e.* to heaven and to hell], my sone ther be,
>Thou hast fre choyse wedur to passe.

Confessio Amantis (E. E. T. S., E. S. 81), p. 218, ll. 3260-3262:

>For every man his oghne wone
>After the lust of his assay
>The vice or vertu chese may.

Hoccleve (E. E. T. S., E. S. 61), p. 112, ll. 73-75:

>for sythen god to man / gyven hathe libertie,
>which chese may / for to do well or no,
>yf he myse-chese / he is his owne foo.

Ibid. p. 215, ll. 18-24, f. a.:

And sikirly, syn god of his hy grace and benigne courtesie hath yeuen vs libertee and freedam for to purchace by oure wirkes in this present lyfe þat oon or þat othir / al standith in our choys and eleccioun! to grete fooles been we / but if we cheese the bettre part / which part, god of his infynyt goodnesse graunte vs alle to cheese / Amen!

Anglia, vii (1884), *Anzeiger*, p. 86, ll. 36-38:

>And of two wayes þou most nedys chese oon.
>Thenk, of fre choyes god hath the ȝeve alon
>With wyt and reson to rule thy lyberte.

This opinion is not only in accordance with *Sirach*, xv, 12-17, but has also been supported as doctrine by great fathers of the Church.

Sirach, xv, 12-17:

12. Non dicas: Ille me implanavit: non enim necessarii sunt ei homines impii. 13. Omne exsecramentum erroris odit Dominus, et non erit amabile timentibus eum. 14. Deus ab initio constituit hominem, et reli-

Notes: Poem I. Pages 7, 8, lines 171-183.   43

quit illum in manu consilii sui. 15. Adjecit mandata et praecepta sua: 16. Si volueris mandata servare, conservabunt te, et in perpetuum fidem placitam facere. 17. Apposuit tibi aquam et ignem : ad quod volueris, porrige manum tuam. 18. Ante hominem vita et mors, bonum et malum : quod placuerit ei, dabitur illi.

Clemens Alexandrinus, Stromatum lib. ii. Sylburg, Coloniae, 1688, 363:

Ἡμεῖς δὲ, οἱ δὲ αἵρεσιν καὶ φυγὴν δεδόσθαι τοῖς ἀνθρώποις αὐτοκρατορικὴν παρὰ τοῦ Κυρίου διὰ τῶν γραφῶν παρειληφότες ἀμεταπτώτῳ τῇ πίστει ἀναπαυώμεθα.

Origines de principiis, interprete Rufino, lib. iii, c. i, Redepenning 245.

"quoniam in ecclesiastica praedicatione inest etiam de futuro Dei justo judicio fides quae judicii credulitas provocat homines et suadet ad bene praeclareque vivendum et omni genere refugere peccatum ... per hoc sine dubio indicatur quod in nostra sit positum potestate vel laudabili nos vitae vel culpabili dedere."

Ibid. lib. iii, c. i, 6 (249):

" Paulus tamquam in nobis ipsis vel salutis vel perditionis habentibus causas, ait: An divitias bonitatis ejus ... contemnis ... ?"

Augustinus, *Hypognosticon*, lib. iii, c. 3 (Migne, *P. lat.*, 45, 1611 ss. = x, 2):

Igitur liberum arbitrium hominibus esse, certa fide credimus, et praedicamus indubitanter.

Thomas Aquinas, *Summa theologica*, i, 23, 3 (Romae 1888, iv.):

"Culpa provenit ex libero arbitrio eius qui reprobatur et a gratia deseritur."

Compare about this difficult matter Schmidt, Wilhelm, *Christliche Dogmatik*, in *Sammlung theologischer Handbücher*, iv, i, 2, Bonn, 1898, § 1, p. 12 ff., and Harnack, Adolf, *Lehrbuch der Dogmengeschichte*, 3. Bd. 3. A. Freiburg i. B., 1897 (*Sammlung theolog. Lehrbücher*), p. 189 ff.

p. 7, l. 171. dismenbre] Compare Skeat, *Chaucer*, vii, ii, 255, and the notes by the same (*ibid.* v) to *C. T.*, C. 474, 651, I. 591, where many quotations on this subject are found. I may only be allowed to add that the ten commandments from which Todd cites the second one are printed by Zupitza in *Herrig's Archiv*, lxxxv (1890), p. 46 ff., from Ashmole MS. 61. Compare also Percy Society, 23, i, 73 :

Of newe tourment we do hym rent,
Whan we lys membres swer.

Hoccleve (E. E. T. S., E. S. 72), p. 23, ll. 628-630:

Þere, þe former of euery creature
Dismembred y with opës grete, & rente
Lyme for lyme, or þat I þennës wente.

l. 179. Compare l. 70.

p. 8, l. 181. nedes—most] Compare note to l. 29.

st. 27. The anacoluthon in this stanza—there is no verb—is nearly as bad as the well-known one at the beginning of Lydgate's *Guy of Warwick*, ed. by Zupitza, *Sitzungsberichte der (Wiener) Kais. Akademie der Wissenschaften*, 74, Wien, 1873, p. 665, note to l. 1, 8. Compare also Skeat, *Chaucer*, i, xiv, l. 1 ff. and note.

p. 8, l. 183. the fadres sapiens] Compare Skeat, *Chaucer*, iv, *C. T.*, B. 1660-1662:

Thurgh thyn [*i. e.* Maria] humblesse, the goost that in thalighte,
Of whos vertu, whan he thyn herte lighte,
Conceived was the fadres sapience.

44 *Notes: Poem I. Page 8, lines* 184–208.

p. 8, ll. 184, 185. well—grounde] See Schick, *T. G.* 292, 293, and note, 754, 758, 971. Also in *Hoccleve* (E. E. T. S., E. S. 72), p. xlix, l. 34.
l. 185. lombe] See Morrill, *Speculum* (E. E. T. S., E. S. 75), note to l. 260.
l. 186. declyne] has here the meaning of 'to die'; see Mätzner and *New English Dictionary*.
l. 195. folow shuld his trace] Skeat, *Chaucer*, i, xiv, 1–4:
> The firste stok, fader of gentilesse—
> What man that claymeth gentil for to be,
> Must folowe his trace, and alle his wittes dresse
> Vertu to sewe, and vyces for to flee.

See also the notes to these lines.
M. P. 93: Who foloweth his tracys is never liche to thryve.
Ibid. 248: To folwe the tracys of spiritual doctryne.
Percy Soc., xiv, 1: *Poems of John Audelay*, ed. by J. O. Halliwell, p. 80:
> To heven to folow the trasse.

Hoccleve (E. E. T. S., E. S. 72), p. 146, l. 4061:
> If þou be god, thow folow most his trace.

Yorkshire Writers, Rolle of Hampole, ii, p. 42, l. 535:
> Synne dos þe to folow þo fendus trace.

196. Compare the last lines of a carol in Percy Society, 23, i, 48:
> And cf owre synnys we ask remyssion,
> And grace
> In hevne to have a place.

l. 208. ouer-terved] Compare about this verb Skeat, *Chaucer*, v, Addenda following p. xxvi, vi, p. 258, and *Athenæum*, 3465 (24. iii. 1894), p. 379. As to its etymology Skeat combines it with the frequentative verb *terflen*, O.E. tearflian (Low G. tarven, um- tarven, O.H.G. zerben, zirben, zirbelwint); Holthausen, *Anglia Beiblatt*, xii, p. 146, refers to *Ettmüller, Ludovicus, Vorda Vealhstôd Engla and Seaxna. Lexicon Anglosaxonicum*. [*Bibliothek der gesammten deutschen National-Literatur*, xxix.] Quedlinburg und Leipzig, 1851, p. 523, *sub* 'teorfan,' and *Schade, Oskar, Altdeutsches Wörterbuch*, 2. A. Halle a. S. 1872–1882, p. 1230, *sub* 'zarbjan.' Holthausen also suggests the idea that 'Tyrfingr,' the icelandic name of a famous sword, belongs to the same root. In *Athenæum*, 3467 (7. iv. 1894), p. 445, F. B. (?) draws the attention to the noun and verb 'turf,' used by labourers in southern and south-western counties for 'piece of ground' and 'strip and roll up layers of rooted grass.'

From the references above mentioned, and the *Century Dictionary*, I collect the following quotations, to which I add some others.

The simple verb *terven* occurs: Skeat, *Chaucer*, iv, *C. T.*, G. 1171, 1274; *Legends of the Holy Rood* (ed. by Morris, E. E. T. S. 46), p. 207; *Havelock* (ed. by Holthausen, Heidelberg, 1900), ll. 603, 918; *Wars of Alexander* (ed. by Skeat, E. E. T. S., E. S. 47), l. 4114; *Alliterative Poems* (ed. by Morris, E. E. T. S. 1), B. 630; *Sir Gawayne and the Green Knight* (ed. by Morris, E. E. T. S. 4), l. 1921; *Prompt. Parv.* sub 'tyrf,' sb.; *The Poems of William Dunbar* (ed. by J. Schipper, Vienna, 1894), 86, l. 23:
> Off all his claythis thay tirvit him bair.

Ibid. ll. 33, 34:
> In tene, thay tirvit him agane,
> And till ane pillar thai him band.

Ibid. l. 57:
> Agane thay tirvit him bak and syd.

The Poems of Walter Kennedy (ed. by J. Schipper, Vienna, 1901, in

Notes: Poem I. Pages 8, 9, lines 210-219. 45

Denkschriften der K. Akademie der Wissenschaften in Wien. Philosophisch-Historische Classe. Band, xlviii, i), p. 87, st. ccvii:
Ane to name wes callit Cleophas,
Said: Merwall is þat þou misknawis allane
Thir cruell dedis quhilum thir dais wes
To Jhesus done into Jerusalem,
Be oure princis how he wes tane [and] slane,
Als tiruit [him] with mony panis fell,
Quhom we trowit to redeme Israell.

ouerterven occurs:
Promptorium Parvulorum (1440), p. 373:
Ovyr (tyr) vyñ (ovyr tyrvyn, K. *ouerturnyn,* S. H. *ouyrturnyn,* P.). Subverto, everto.

J. Hardyng, *Chron. of England* (ed. Ellis, 1812), p. 47:
So dred they hym, they durst no thing ouer terue
Againe his lawe nor peace.

Ibid. p. 75:
The lawe and peace he kepte, and conserued,
Which him vpheld, that he was neuer ouer terued.

Jamieson, John, *An Etymological Dictionary of the Scottish Language,* ii, Edinburgh, 1841, p. 173:
Reprowyd scho suld noucht be for-thi
Of falshede, or of trychery,
For til owrtyrwe that is abowe.—
Bot qwhen thai trayst hyr all thair best,
All that is gywyn be that Lady,
Scho owrtyrwys it suddanly.   Wyntown, viii, 40, 39, 46.

Holland's *Buke of the Houlate,* ed. by Arthur Diebler, Leipzig, 1893, ll. 836-839:
The golk gat vp agane in þe grit hall,
Tit þe tuquheit be þe tope and owirtirwit his heid,
Flang him flat in þe fyre, fedderis and all.

Hoccleve (E. E. T. S., E. S. 72), l. 1811:
Wolde honest deth come, and me ouerterue.

I think 'ouerterve' occurs once also in Skeat, *P. P.* (E. E. T. S. 28), A. ix, ll. 30, 31:
For ȝif he ne rise þe raþer · and rauhte to þe steorne,
þe wynt wolde with þe water · þe Bot ouer-þrowe.[1]

p. 8, l. 210. they] *i.e.* the eight souls; 'world'=mankind. I think, we cannot refrain from supplying "were" to render the construction clear: 'and they were preserved.'

p. 9, l. 213. maner] used without 'of'; see Skeat, *Chaucer,* vi, p. 159, and v, p. 176, note to l. 1689; Mätzner, *Englische Grammatik,*[3] Berlin, 1885, iii, p. 338.

219. As for a tyme] 'as' is here used pleonastically, without proper meaning, as it fairly often occurs before adverbs; compare Schick, *T. G.,* note to l. 39, and the note to H., ll. 186, 368, 371; also Prof. F. J. Child's *Observations on the Language of Chaucer and Gower* in Ellis, *On Early English Pronunciation,* ch. iv, § 5 (E. E. T. S., E. S. 27), p. 374. I noticed further:
M. P. 63:
Folowyng these baladis as for your plesaunce.

[1] ouertorne H₂ [= ouertorue?]

Ibid. 196 : Coold and moist, as of his nature.
Ibid. 257 : Oonly outward as by apparence.
Schleich, *Fabula*, 41, 42 :
    Anothir marchaunt, as by relacioun,
    Of hym hadde herd and of his high renoun.
Ibid. p. 70, where some other quotations are found.
Steele, *Secrees*, 1595, 1596 :
    Off which as by Age / Oon is natural,
    The othir by fortune / As be thynges accidental.
Falls, 91 a 1 :
    And leuer he had his father toffende,
    As in such case than through negligence,
    vnto his goddes for to do offence.
G. W. (Robinson), 493 :
    As ffor a tyme to holde with hym soiour.
Skeat, *Chaucer,* vii, xxi, 74 :
    So must me nedes abyde, as for a space.
Ibid. vii, iv, 120, 121 :
    For-thy, my worthy prince, in Cristes halve,
    As for a part whos fayth thou hast to gyde.
Ibid. iv, *C. T.*, B. 122, 123 :
    O riche marchaunts, ful of wele ben ye,
    O noble, o prudent folk, as in this cas !
Ibid. iv, *C. T.*, E. 404–406 :
    That to Janicle, of which I spak bifore,
    She doghter nas, for, as by coniecture,
    Hem thoughte she was another creature.
Percy Society, xi, ii : *Thirteen Psalms,* p. 24 :
    The heavens also, as with a thought,
    Thou havest set vp with all theire light.
Hoccleve (E. E. T. S., E. S. 72), p. 13, ll. 344, 345 :
    Was it not eek a monstre as in nature
    þat god I-borë was of a virgine?
Confessio Amantis (E. E. T. S., E. S. 81, 82), i, 1940, 2765 ; ii, 76 ; iii, 1122 ; iv, 1181, 1651 ; v, 750, 6547 ; viii, 1297.

    p. 9, l. 221. boght derre] See Morrill, *Speculum,* note to l. 160.
    l. 223. Then] = than. The structure of this phrase is entirely Lydgatian. l. 222 L. begins : 'Ley to thy sore—this same salfe . . . .' but his beloved parenthesis : '& let no-thing lye nerre' puts him out, and he inconsistently goes on : 'Then (= than) this same salfe.' Evidently, the scribe of C was not satisfied by this phrase and tried to improve it by inserting 'that' after 'Ley,' l. 222.
    with] postponed preposition.
    ll. 225, 226. These two lines recall the beginning of the Parson's Tale : Skeat, *Chaucer,* iv, *C. T.*, I. § 1 : 'Our swete lord god of hevene, that no man wole perisse, but wole that we comen alle to the knoweleche of him, and to the blisful lyf that is perdurable, amonesteth us by the prophete Ieremie.'
    A very similar passage occurs, *Pilgr.* 8591–94 :
        But, off that lord grettest off myght,
        Whos mercy euer passeth ryht,
        Off synnerys desyreth nat the deth ;
        ffor he doth mercy or that he sleth.

p. 9. l. 231. queme & plese] Compare Schick, *T. G.* 1312 and note to this line, and Schleich, *Fabula*, l. 147 and p. 127.
   p. 10, l. 243. It is preferable to follow C and to omit 'the,' though we could take it as 'dativus ethicus'; compare Spies, *Studien*, § 152.
   l. 244. *Ayenbite of Inwit*, ed. by R. Morris (E. E. T. S. 23), p. 154 : Þet habbeþ zuo þe herten engriued ine þe dyeueles nette / ase zayþ Iob.
   l. 250. Dispose] Steele, *Secrees*, 595 :
      Dispose them sylff / to mornyng or to gladnesse.
   l. 256. to-togged and to-drawe] As to the signification of the prefix *to-* compare Skeat, *Chaucer*, v, note to B. l. 3215, and vii, note to xviii, l. 137. In H., l. 127, occurs ' to-Rent.'
   l. 260. *Pilgr.* 2899, 2900 :
      Whan God Almyghty (yiff yt be souht,)
      Al thys world hadde maad off nouht.
   Ibid. 6603, 6604 :
      " God the ffader," fful wel ywrouht,
      That heuene and erthë made off nouht.
   Hoccleve (E. E. T. S., E. S. 72), p. 13, ll. 341, 342 :
      Schal he rebelle ageyn his lordës myght,
      Which þat þis wydë world haþ made of noght.
   Percy Society, vii, 2 : *A Paraphrase on the seven penitential psalms, in English verse*, ed. by W. H. Black, p. 7 :
      Zyf God, that made all thyng of nouȝt.
   Yorkshire Writers, Rolle of Hampole ii, p. 41, l. 431 :
      þi-sclue, mon, he made of noght.
   Ibid. p. 102, l. 10 f. b. :
      god þat made the of nought.
   The Poems of William Dunbar, ed. by J. Schipper, Vienna, 1894, p. 350, No. 78, ll. 107, 108 :
      . . . ., Man, lufe the Lord most deir,
      That the and all this warld maid of nocht.
   l. 262. cesede] = put an end to.
   l. 267. adolescens] The earliest quotation of this word in the *New English Dictionary* is from Lydgate's *Bochas*, 1554 (*i. e.* ca. 1430). Again, I found it in *Manipulus Vocabulorum*, by Peter Levins (1570), ed. by H. B. Wheatley [E. E. T. S. 27.], London, 1867, col. 96, l. 26 : A'dolescencie, *adolescentia, œ*. The Dictionaries by Mätzner, Stratmann-Bradley, the *Century Dictionary*, and the Index to Chaucer's works by Skeat, vi and vii, do not give any quotation. I noticed it once, but in the Latin form, in *Anglia*, xiv, p. 496 :
      When adolescencia is auncient & cūmyth to gravite.
   p. 11, l. 272. weyes . . . of your youth] *Anglia*, vii (1884), *Anzeiger*, p. 85, ll. 3, 4 :
      Thow mynly myrroure yn whom all old may se
      The wayes of youth yn whych they have mysgoon.
   l. 273. For] See note to l. 74.
   kowthe] Though assonance is not unknown in Lydgate (see Schick, *T. G.*, p. lx, and Schleich, *Fabula*, p. lxvii), we think it preferable to read, against the MSS., 'kowthe.'
   l. 281. *Falls*, 3 b. 1 :
      For vnto a man that perfit is and stable.
   l. 285. notheles] evidently refers to ll. 281, 282.

48   Notes: Poem I. Page 11, 12, lines 293-305.

p. 11, l. 293. Compare Schick, T. G., note to l. 191, and Krausser, Complaint, note to l. 484.

l. 294. Vnkyndly] = unnatural, against nature. Compare Falls, 20 a 1:
who search aright was vnkindly mariage,
speaking about Oedipus.

Ibid. 20 a 1:
also of her (i. e. Iocaste) sonnes the great vnkyndness, because one brother murdered the other.

Ibid. 23 a 1:
Bloud vnto bloud to shew vnkindnes,
in the story of Atreus and Thyestes.

Percy Soc. 28: Poems of William de Shoreham, ed. by T. Wright, p. 115:

And sodomyt hys senne
Aȝens kende y-do.

Ayenbite of Inwyt, ed. by R. Morris (E. E. T. S. 23), p. 9:
Ine þise heste is uorbode / alle zennen a-ye kende / ine huet manere / hy byeþ y-do / oþer ine his bodie : oþer in oþren.

Confessio Amantis (E. E. T. S., E. S. 81), p. 236, ll. 373-375:
And for he [i. e. Tiresias] hath destourbed kindᴈ
And was so to nature unkinde,
Unkindeliche he was transformed.

In this meaning the word occurs still in Shakespeare. Venus and Adonis, ed. by Delius, p. 13:
O! had thy mother borne so hard a mind,
She had not brought forth thee, but died unkind.

Delius remarks: unkind = unnatural, contrary to the laws of nature, which bid the wives to bring forth children.

Compare l. 301, and also ll. 33 and 36.

l. 301. vnkyndly] See note to l. 294.

p. 12, l. 302. The fende, youre enmye] M. P. 97:
The fiende oure enemye outraye and confounde.

lying in a-wayte] Pilgr. 64, 65:
And deth, ay redy with hys dart to kerue,
Lyth in a-wayt, dredful off manacys.

Ibid. 4491: In a-wayt y (i. e. Penance) lygge alway.

Ibid. 8130, 8131:
Ther lyth A mortal hunteresse,
In a-wayt to hyndre the.

S. of Thebes, 359 b 1:
That on this hill, like as I conceiue,
Liest in a waite, folkes to deceiue.

Ibid. 364 b 1: By false engine, ligging in a weite.

Falls, 212 b 2: The people alway in a wayte lying.

Rom. of the R. 4497:
Which in awayte lyth day and night.

Hoccleve (E. E. T. S., E. S. 72), p. 137, l. 3806:
The fend lyth in a-wayte of oure freelte.

ll. 304, 305. lynes—hokes] Schleich, Fabula, 740:
He wolde, that deth had leyd hook and lyne.

There are many quotations to this line found ibid. on p. 102. We add Falls, 95 a 1:

Notes: Poem I. Pages 12, 13, lines 308–336.

        hym to betraishe she cast out hoke and lyne.
p. 12, l. 308. Compare *Introduction*, § 6.
l. 311. confusioun] = ruin, perdition, as in the Bible. Compare *Falls*, 140 b 1 :
        And ouercome for his great pride,
        At great mischief to his confusion.
Ibid. 173 b 2 : For thei not knew to theyr confusion,
        Time of their notable visitacion.
M. P. 5 :   Alltho that bethe enmyes to the Kyng,
        I schalle hem clothe withe confusione.
Schick, *T. G.* 228 :
        A man to loue to his confusioun.
Compare also the note to this line.
Rom. of the R. 3833, 3834 :
        To truste (to thy confusioun)
        Him thus, . . .
Hoccleve (E. E. T. S., E. S. 61), p. 145, l. 154 :
        My deeth wole it been, & confusion.
l. 317. strenght] instead of 'strength.' Compare Schleich, *Fabula*, p. lii, below.
l. 318. Yf] temporal.
l. 324. here] = on earth, in this life.
p. 13, l. 335.
M. P. 239 :   S. our Savacioun, whan we shal hens weende.
Ibid. :   Do mercy Ihesu! or that we hens pace.
Ibid. 240 :   Or I passe hens, this hoolly myn entent.
Ibid. 249 :   Or I passe hens, Ihesu, graunt unto me.
Voss., *Gg.* 9, fol. 108 b :
        Thynk how that thi-self shall henne.
l. 336. *M. P.* 229 :   The secounde schyle ys that thou shalle dye,
        Bote ȝyt what tyme thou woste never.
Voss., *Gg.* 9, f. 35 b :
        For deth cometh ever whan men list (*i. e.* least) on him thynk.
Percy Society, vii : *A paraphrase on the seven penitential psalms, in English verse*, ed. by W. H. Black, p. 32 (and note on p. 64), st. lxxxiii, ll. 5, 6 :
        My deth evermore in mynde I kepe ;
        I wote noȝt whanne myn ende schal be.
Hoccleve (E. E. T. S., E. S. 72), p. 21, ll. 566, 567 :
        No thyng is morë certein þan deþ is,
        Ne more vncertein þan þe tyme I-wis.
Ibid. p. 105, ll. 2893, 2894 :
        Remembreth euer a-monge, þat ye shul dye,
        And wot naght whan ; it comeþ in a stelthe.
Ibid. (E. E. T. S., E. S. 61), p. 67, ll. 7, 8 :
        Þat dye I sholde / & hadde no knowynge
        Whanne, ne whidir, I sholde hennes sterte.
Ibid., p. 117, l. 210 :
        war that / for deathe comethe, wot ther no wyght whan.
Political, Religious, and Love Poems, ed. by F. J. Furnivall (E. E. T. S. 15), p. 108, ll. 169, 170 :
        Þou kepe me, lorde, for I sal dye,
        & wot neuere whore, ne how, ne when.

Ibid. p. 221, *Three Certainties of the Day of Death* :

> Hit beoþ þreo tymes on þo day
> þat soþe to witen me mai :
> þat on ys, þat i shal henne ;
> þat oþer, þat y not whenne ;
> þat þridde is my moste care,
> þat y not whider i shal fare.

Yorkshire Writers, Rolle of Hampole, i, p. 367, viii, 17, 18 :
With I. and E., þe dede to þe sall come als I þe kene,
Bot þou ne wate in whate-kyn state, ne how, ne whare, ne whenne.
Ibid., i, p. 106, ll. 12-14 f. a. :
An other thynge is the vncertaynte of our endynge / for we wote not whan we shall dye nor how we shall dye nor whether we shall goo whan we be deed.

p. 13, l. 339. can] See note to l. 54.
l. 343. which] See note to l. 141.
whoso] Compare Schick, *T. G.*, note to l. 1090, and e. g. *M. P.* 3, 8, 15, 69, 97, 137, etc.

l. 357. *Margarete*, 540 :
> And be her shelde in myschief and dissese.

l. 361. werre or stryfe] one of Lydgate's favourite expressions. Compare Degenhart, *Hors*, 405 :
> Lat al werre and stryfe be sette aside.

Ibid. 410 : Of newe stryf and of mortal werre.
M. P. 85 : Whiche for vertue, without werre and stryff.
Pilgr. 1968 : With-outen werre or any stryff.
S. of Thebes, 359 b 1 :
> Muse herevpon, without warre of [*sic !* or ?] strife

Ibid. 360 a 2 : Edippus aie, deuoide of warre and strife.
Ibid. 361 a 1 : Finde plentie of conteke, warre and strife.
Ibid. 372 b 1 : Replenished, with conteke werre and strife.
It occurs also Skeat, *Chaucer*, iv, *C. T.*, F. 757 :
> As in my gilt, were outher werre or stryf.

Hoccleve (E. E. T. S., E. S. 72), p. 182, l. 5041 :
> Euene as a man is euer in werre and strife.

Ibid. p. 195, l. 5405 :
> Now, pees ! approche, and dryue out werre & strif !

Ibid. (E. E. T. S., E. S. 61), p. 34, l. 302 :
> Malencolie engendrith werre & stryfe.

Confessio Amantis (E. E. T. S., E. S. 81), p. 11, l. 248 :
> Hath set to make werre and strif.

Ibid. (E. E. T. S., E. S. 82), p. 122, l. 6414* :
> Upon knyhthode in werre and strif.

Ibid. p. 257, l. 900 :
> And desirous of werre and strif.

p. 14, l. 374. We follow here the reading of C and insert 'all' : 'of all trewth,' because it makes the metre so much better.
l. 384. in-to] e and o are much alike in our manuscript, as is also pointed out by Schleich, *Fabula*, p. xliii.
l. 385. Longens] Compare Gattinger, p. 39, and Skeat, *Chaucer*, i, 1, 163 note. This proper name occurs also e. g. *Kk.* i, fol. 195 b, 198 a.
l. 388. *Kk.* i, 195 b :

Consummatum est // seyde whan all was do.
Compare *Introduction*, § 6.
 p. 15, l. 393. Compare Skeat, *Chaucer*, iv, *C. T.*, A. 981 :
  Thus rit this duk, thus rit this conquerour.
 l. 395. can] See note to l. 54.
 l. 397. hert, wyll, & thought] Another stereotype expression. Compare *Flour of Curtesye*, 248 b 1 :
  Yet or I die, with hert, wil, and thought.
 Degenhart, *Hors*, 510 :
  Ondevided, with herte, wil, and thouht.
 Margaret, 204 :
  Quod she ageyn: with hert, wille and thoughte.
 Also in Skeat, *Chaucer*, vii, xxiv, 205 :
  Caitif and wrecche in hert, in wille, and thought!
 Ibid. 426 :
  Clere of entent, and herte, and thought and wille.
 l. 398. Skeat, *Chaucer*, vii, xi, 43 :
  Now, lady myn! sith I you love and drede.
 Hoccleve (E. E. T. S., E. S. 72), p. 105, l. 2898 :
  Hym [*i. e.* God], loue & drede ; and his lawës obeyeth.
 Political, Religious, and Love Poems, ed. by F. J. Furnivall (E. E. T. S. 15), p. 108, l. 156 :
  & fe[r]uently þe lufe and drede.
 Ibid. p. 251, ll. 6, 7 :
  Good god! þou graunt me þis,
  That I may lyue in loue & drede.
 l. 400. *Kk.* i, f. 195 a :
  Helle robbed // thourgh myn jmperial mygt.
 ll. 411–413. It is quite common to close a poem, especially a spiritual one, with a prayer. We find this custom, *e. g.* in *M. P.* 58, 66, 73, 179, 232 ; *Giles*, 329–368 ; *Edmund*, ii, 1457–1520 (again, p. 445, ll. 457–464); *Margarete*, 534–540 ; *Anglia*, vii (1884), *Anzeiger*, p. 86, ll. 53–58 ; Skeat, *Chaucer*, ii, *Troilus*, v, 1860–1869 ; *ibid.* i, 1, 181–184.
 Also in many poems in *Publications of the Percy Society*, iv, 1.
 l. 413. *M. P.* 198 :
  Toward that lyf wher joye is ay lastyng.
 Ibid. 220 : With hym to dwelle above the sterrys cleere.

POEM II.

 p. 16, l. 1. Titan] See note to c. l. 26. Compare also the opening line in Triggs, *Assembly;* Skeat, *Chaucer*, iii, table I, and Schick, *T. G.*, Introduction, p. cxxii f.
 l. 2. Even] Here, and l. 38, it means 'evening,' and is not an expression of space, as l. 344, but of time.
 Saphyre-huwed sky] Lydgate's predilection for alluding to jewelry is well known ; compare Schick, *T. G.*, p. cxvi, note, and l. 259, note, and in our poem, ll. 33, 34, 362. Compare also *Kk.* i, fol. 199 a :
  Charboncle of Chastite / & grene Emeroude stoon.

Notes: Poem II. Page 16, Lines 4–5.

Ibid.: O sapher, lowþe / all swellyng to represse.
Ibid.: The Cristal Cloystre / of þy Virginite.
M. P. 181, 183, 188, 190, 191, 222.
Æsop (Sauerstein), i, 23:
   Riche saphyrs, and rubyes, ful royal.
p. 16, l. 4. Compare Skeat, *Chaucer*, iv, *C. T.*, A. 9:
   And smale fowles maken melodye.
Steele, *Secrees*, 1308:
   The bryddys syngen / in their Armonye.
See in our poem, l. 357.
 l. 5. sugred] A favourite expression of Lydgate when speaking of music or poetry. Compare Koeppel, *De casibus virorum illustrium*, p. 46, and note 3, and in our poem, l. 354.
Steele, *Secrees*, 1309:
   Salwe that sesoun / with sugryd mellodye.
Ibid. 220:
   Thorugh his sugryd / Enspyred Elloquence,
and note to this line.
M. P. 11:   For to practyse withe sugrid melody.
Ibid. 25:   Where is Tullius with his sugrid tonge.
Ibid. 102:   Ambrosius withe sugred eloquence.
Ibid. 150:   Speche is but fooly and sugryd elloquence.
Ibid. 182:   And the soote sugred armonye.
S. of Thebes (Wülcker), p. 106, l. 52:
   By rehearsaile of his sugred mouthe.
Falls 32 a 1:   And for his sote sugred armonie.'
Ibid. 69 a 1:   With many a colour of sugred eloquence.
Pilgr. 176, 177:
   Nor I drank no-wer of the sugryd tonne
   Off Iubiter, . . .
as an excuse for his 'rudenesse.'
 l. 5. complyne] See note to c., l. v.—About the idea of 'divine service sung by birds,' compare Neilson, William Allan, *The Origins and Sources of the Court of Love* in *Studies and Notes in Philology and Literature*, vi [Harvard University], Boston, 1899. Here an entire chapter, vi, p. 216 ff., is devoted to the investigation of the 'Birds' Matins,' and especially, p. 225 ff., sub C., examples of 'Parodies sung by birds' are collected: *La Messe des Oisiaus* of Jean de Condé (Scheler, *Dits et Contes*, iii, 1 ff.); *Devotions of the Fowles* of John Lydgate (*M. P.* 78 ff.); *A Proper New Boke of the Armonye of Byrdes* (Percy Society, vii); *Cuckoo and the Nightingale* (Skeat, *Chaucer*, vii, 350); *The Golden Targe* of Dunbar (Scottish Text Society, ii, 1–10; Schipper, 17, 100–113); *Testament of Squyer Meldrum* of Lindesay (E. E. T. S. 35, 1868, p. 371). Compare A. Jeanroy in *Revue crit. d'hist. et de lit.*, 1901, 51, pp. 272–3. Some other examples are noted in Skeat, *Chaucer*, vii, p. 552: *Chaucer, Parl. of Foules*, and *Dunbar, Thistle and Rose*.
 I may be allowed to add some others:
M. P. 182:   Esperus enforced hir corage,
     Toward evyn whan Phebus gan to west,
     And the braunches to hir avauntage,
     To syng hir complyn and than go to rest.
Ibid. 242:   The amerous fowlys with motetys and carollys,
     Salwe that sesoun every morwenyng.

Skeat, *Chaucer* i, iii : *The Book of the Duchesse,* ll. 294–304 :
> [I] loked forth, for I was waked
> With smale foules a gret hepe,
> . . . . . .
> . . . . . .
> And songen, everich in his wyse,
> The moste solempne servyse
> By note, that ever man, I trowe,
> Had herd ; . . .

Ibid. vii, p. 374, xx : *Flower and Leaf,* ll. 435–437 :
> For then the nightingale, that al the day
> Had in the laurer sete, and did her might
> The hool servyse to sing longing to May.

The Owl and the Nightingale, ed. by Wright (Percy Society, xi), p. 41, ll. 1177–1180 :
> For prestes wike ich wat thu dest,
> Ich not ȝef thu were ȝavre prest ;
> Ich not ȝef thu canst masse singe,
> I-noh thu canst of mansinge.

Also in Holland's *Buke of the Houlate,* ed. by Diebler, Leipzig, 1893, p. 44, st. 55 ff., birds are singing a ghostly song in the praise of the Virgin Mary.

p. 16, l. 6. Compare Skeat, *Chaucer,* iv., *C. T.*, A. 11 :
> So priketh hem nature in hir corages.

Ibid. i, v, 324, 325 :
> and than the foules smale,
> That eten as hem nature wolde enclyne.

Æsop (Sauerstein), ii, 58 :
> As he (*i. e.* the cock) was taught only by nature.

M. P. 157 : Alle othir beestys obeye at his biddyng,
> As kynde hath tauhte hem, ther lady and maistresse.

Ibid. 237 : Foulys, beestys, and fisshes of the se,
> Kynde hath tauhte hem by natural disciplyne,
> Meekly to Ihesu to bowe adoun ther kne.

l. 7. hem] = themselves. Here and ll. 158 and 261 (it, hym) the personal pronoun is used as reflexive pronoun ; compare Spies, *Studien,* p. 152 f. and p. 169.

l. 8. Compare *M. P.* 145 :
> Yif he hadde sithe tyme that he was born.

Kk. i, fol. 197 a :
> Fro þat tyme / þat y was bore.

Schick, *T. G.* 1376, 1377 :
> Bicause I had neuer in my life aforne
> Sei[n] none so faire, fro time þat I was borne.

Pilg. 3259, 3260 :
> Mor merveyllous than euere aforn
> I hadde seyn syth I was born.

Ibid. 3309, 3310 :
> Mor than euere I was a-fore,
> Syth tymë that I was bore.

Also *Amis and Amiloun,* ed. Kölbing, 1955, 1956 :
> Þe best bourd, bi mi leute,
> Þou herdest, seþþen þou were born !

p. 16, l. 9. downe nor daale] A very common alliterative expression; compare Mätzner.

l. 10. thorne] The nightingale is very often described as sitting on a thorn. I need not deal with this question here, as the reader will find in Dr. Schick's note to l. ii, 2, 50 of his new edition of *Kyd's Spanish Tragedy*, how familiar to poets this idea was throughout mediæval literature. Compare ll. 61, 356 of our poem.

l. 14. refreyd] In *Century Dictionary* I find:
refrait: Same as refrain² [= The musical phrase or figure to which the burden of a song is set.]
the refraite of his laye salewed the kynge Arthur and the Quene Gonnore, and alle the other after.—*Merlin* (E. E. T. S. 36, 112), p. 615, l. 19.
It occurs again: *ibid.* p. 310, l. 11:
entende what songe thei seiden, saf that thei seiden in refreite of hir songe.

The word is also mentioned by J. O. Halliwell in his *Dictionary of Archaisms and Provincialisms*, London, 1846-7:
refret: The burden of a song.
    This was the refret of that caroull, y wene,
    The wheche Gerlen and this mayden song byfore.
        Chron. Vilodun. p. 115.

I found it also in Skeat, *Chaucer*, vii: *The Testament of Love*, iii, i, 156 (and note):
For ever sobbinges and complayntes be redy refrete in his meditacions, as werbles in manifolde stoundes comming about I not than.

l. 14. Occy] See c. l. 90 and note.
l. 16. ledne] Compare Schick, *T. G.* 139 and note, and Skeat, *Chaucer*, v, note to F. 435. *The Poems of William Dunbar*, ed. by J. Schipper, Vienna, 1894, p. 157, No. 28, l. 106:
    Bot it sowld be all trew Scottismennis leid.

Percy Society, 28: *The Poems of William de Shoreham*, ed. by T. Wright, p. 10:
    And onderstand hi more bi sed
      In alle manere speche,
        Ine lede.

Skeat, *P. P.*, C. xiv, 173; xv, 179; B. xii, 244, 253, 262.
Drayton, *Polyolbion*, xii, 503 (from *Century Dictionary*):
    The ledden of the birds most perfectly she knew.

Fragm. in Warton, *History of English Poetry* (1824), i, p. 24:
    And halp thor he sag mikel ned
    Biddi hie singen non other led.

Debate of the Body and the Soul (Appendix to *Mapes's Poems*, ed. by Wright, Camden Society, 1841), p. 334, l. 11:
    ʒwere is al thi michele pride, and thi lede that was so loud?
(The two last quotations are taken from *Coleridge's Dictionary*.)
Compare also Reiffenberg, *Chronique rimée de Philippe Mouskes*, Bruxelles, 1838, ii, p. cclix, l. 99:
    Chante li lossignos qui dist en son latin.

(on)] must be omitted, though both MSS. read so, because it disturbs the clear sense of the phrase.

ll. 17, 18. false lovers] Schick, *T. G.* 167, 168:
    On double louers, þat loue þingis nwe,
    Thurgh whos falsnes hindred be þe trwe

Ibid. 215, 216:
>And oþer saugh I ful oft wepe & wring,
>[That they in men founde swych variynge].

and the notes to these lines; Skeat, *Chaucer*, vii, **xxiv**, 575 ff. :
>With dolefull chere, full fele in their complaint
>Cried 'Lady Venus, rewe upon our sore!
>. . . . .
>And ponish, Lady, grevously, we pray,
>The false untrew with counterfet plesaunce,
>That made their oth, be trew to live or dey,
>With chere assured, and with countenaunce;
>And falsly now thay foten loves daunce,
>Barein of rewth, untrue of that they seid,
>Now that their lust and plesire is alleyd.'

p. 16, l. 19. can] See note to c. l. 54.
l. 20. sle] See note to c. l. 90.
p. 17, l. 22. *Falls*, 71 b 1 : To shewe exaumple to folkes in certeine.
l. 24 ff. Similarly twice in Schick, *T. G.* 440 ff. :
>For vnto ȝow his hert I shal so lowe,
>Wiþ-oute spot of eny doubelnes,
>That he ne shal escape fro þe bowe—
>Thouȝ þat him list þuruȝ vnstidfastnes—
>I mene of Cupide, þat shal him so distres
>Vnto your hond, wiþ þe arow of gold,
>That he ne shal escapen þouȝ he would.

Again, *ibid.* 834 ff. :
>And ȝov·I prai of routh and eke pite,
>O goodli planet, o ladi Venus briȝt,
>That ȝe ȝoure sone of his deite—
>Cupid I mene, þat wiþ his dredful myȝt
>And wiþ his brond, þat is so clere of liȝte,
>Hir hert[e] so to fire and to mark,
>As ȝe me whilom brent[e] *with* a spark.

l. 24. parde] A very common, petty oath; compare Skeat, *Chaucer*, vii, p. 530, note to l. 47; and Lange, Hugo, *Die Versicherungen bei Chaucer*. *Diss.*, 1892, Berlin, p. 11 ff.

l. 32 ff. Compare another passage describing the Castle of Love which occurs Skeat, *Chaucer*, vii, xxiv, 69 ff. :
>'At Citheron, sir,' seid he, 'without dowte,
>The King of Love, and all his noble rowte,
>Dwelling within a castell ryally.'
>. . . . .
>No saphir ind, no rubè riche of price,
>There lakked than, nor emeraud so grene,
>Baleis Turkeis, ne thing to my devise.

l. 33. Dungeoun] is not, in this case, identical with 'tower, dungeon,' but has here the general meaning 'habitation, dwelling-place.' Compare *M. P.* 176:
>Diogenes lay in a smal dongoun.

Court of Sapience, e 3 a :
>Than from the dongeon grete within the place
>A solempne towre whiche styed vp to heuen.

Voss. Gg. 9, fol. 79 b. :
>Whan that he slept in his Roiall dongoun.

S. of Thebes, 365 a 1 :
>Till he atteined hath / the chief dongeon
>Where as the kyng / helde his mansion.

Yorkshire Writers, Rolle of Hampole, i, p. 363, ll. 9, 10 :
>Fra a myrke downgcone þou broghte me righte,
>þat es my modirs wambe, to þis lighte.

Ibid. p. 372, ll. 15-17 :
>And my modir consayued me
>In mekill syne and caytefete.
>Than duelled mane in a dongeowne.

p. 17, l. 34. Fret] Compare Kittredge, *Authorship of the English Romaunt of the Rose* in *Studies and Notes in Philology and Literature* (Harvard University), 1. 1892, p. 46, to which we add the following quotations:
Falls, 127 a 1 (also 128 b 2) :
>Forged of gold, fret full of stones clere.

Ibid. 169 a 1 :
>Tables of yuor fret with perre ryche.

S. of Thebes, 363 a 1 :
>Two mantels / vnto hem were brought
>Frette with perle / and riche stones wrought.

Voss. Gg. 9, fol. 76 b :
>All off goold fret with perlis ffyn.

l. 38. Eve] See p. 16, l. 2.

sterris] *S. of Thebes*, 361 b 2 :
>A large space, that the sterres clere
>The cloudes voided, in heuen did appere.

l. 38. dide appere] 'do' is here, and later on, used not in the causative sense of 'make,' but as a simple auxiliary. Compare Lounsbury, *Studies in Chaucer*, ii, 72 ff. and Kaluza, *Chaucer u. der Rosenroman*, Berlin, 1893, p. 40 f.

Steele, *Secrees*, 1296, 1297 :
>What tyme the sesoun / is Comyng of the yeer,
>The hevenly bawme / Ascendyng from the Roote.

l. 39. Similarly, Skeat, *Chaucer*, vii, xx, 5, 6 :
>Causing the ground, felë tymes and oft,
>Up for to give many an hoolsom air.

l. 40. Rede and white] The most common colours of flowers. Compare Krausser, *Complaint*, 1, 2 :
>In May, when Flora, the fressh[e] lusty quene,
>The soyle hath clad in grene, rede, and white.

M. P. 244 :
>With hire chapirlettys greene, whit, and reede.

Ibid. 245 :
>Of thes blosmys, som blew, rede, and white.

S. of Thebes (Skeat), 1244 :
>Vpon the herbes grene, white, & red.

Steele, *Secrees*, 1370 :
>Chapelettys be maad / of Roosys whyte and Rede

Skeat, *Chaucer*, iv, *C. T.*, A. 90 :
>Al ful of fresshe floures, whyte and rede.

Ibid. vii, xiii, 9, 10 :

Also these fresshe somer-floures
Whyte and rede, blewe and grene.
Ibid. xx, 333; xxiv, 1385; etc.
See also Gattinger, p. 65.
  p. 17, ll. 41, 42. Schick, *T. G.* 13, 14 (and note):
Til at[te] last, er I gan taken kepe,
Me did oppresse a sodein dedeli slepe.
Court of Sapience, A. 3 b:
Whyles at the last I fell vpon a slepe.
l. 49. and] Taking it from A., we get a much better metre.
p. 18, l. 50. list] See note to c. l. 9.
l. 51. vnclose] *Pilgr.* 1511, 1512:
Wych to tellyn I purpose,
And a-noon to yow vnclose.
M. P. 25: Of morall Senec, the misteries to unclose.
Schleich, *Fabula,* 361:
To me vncloose the somme of your desyre.
And *ibid.* note on p. 147.
l. 52. cast] = to fix the mind upon, intend, purpose. So in *M. P.* 182:
And in al haste he cast for to make,
Within his house a pratie litelle cage.
Voss. Gg. 9, fol. 71 a:
He cast hym nat to pay no trewage.
S. of Thebes, 374 a 2:
From which appointment we caste vs nat to varie.
Compare also Degenhart, *Hors,* note to l. 504.
ll. 52, 53. nat-Nothyng] Double negation; very common in Middle-English. The sense is nevertheless negative; see ll. 82, 172. Compare Spies, *Studien,* § 240.
l. 53. gardyn of the Rose] *i. e.* as it is described in the *Romaunt of the Rose.* The meaning is: Thou shalt not hear of love-poetry, like that of the *Romaunt of the Rose,* but of religious poetry. Compare Schick, *Kleine Lydgatestudien,* i, in *Anglia,* Beiblatt 8 (1898), p. 134 ff.
l. 55. occy] See note to c. l. 90.
l. 56. she] refers to 'briddis,' l. 55; compare note to c. l. 103.
l. 59. Occy] see note to c. l. 90.
l. 60. lorne] = missed it. The sense is: Many lovers did not understand the deeper meaning of the nightingale's song; they always interpreted her tunes in a secular sense.
l. 61. among] Here, and l. 76, it is an adverb, having the meaning 'sometimes, often.' Compare Ellis, *E. E. P.* i, p. 374, and Morrill, *Speculum* (E. E. T. S., E. S. 75), note to l. 186. I add the following quotations:
Kk. i, f. 194 b:
Remembre among // vpon my passion.
Falls, 3 b 2: voyde auarice and thinke euer among
to his neighbour, that he doe no wrong.
Ibid. 9 b 1: And Cadmus thus toforne Appollo stoode
kneling among with ful great reuerence.
Skeat, *Chaucer,* vii, x, 85, 86:
O ruby, rubifyed in the passioun,
Al of thy sone, among have us in minde.

Ibid. vii, xxi, 300:
>Here wil I stande, awaytinge ever among.

Hoccleve (E. E. T. S., E. S. 72), p. 105, l. 2893:
>Remembreth euer a-monge, þat ye shul dye.

Confessio Amantis (E. E. T. S., E. S. 81), p. 99, l. 2333:
>And evere among he gan to loute.

thorne] See note to l. 10.

p. 18, l. 62. fyry] 'fayre,' as we find in H., is too colourless, wherefore I adopt the reading of A.

l. 64. Compare *S. of Thebes*, 365 a 2:
>The cause fully, that we haue on honde.

Pilgr. 1221, 1222:
>Touchyng that we have on honde,
>Thow must pleynly vnderstonde.

Skeat, *Chaucer*, iv, *C. T.*, E. 1686:
>Of mariage, which we have on honde.

ll. 68–70. Compare for the idea expressed in these lines Schick, *T. G.*, note to l. 450.

l. 70. maner] See note to c. l. 213.

l. 71. Takestow] This emendation surely represents the original reading; afterwards it was wrongly separated by the scribes.

ll. 72, 73. she—hir-self—hir] refer to 'bridde,' l. 71; compare note to c. l. 103.

ll. 72–75. Compare Krausser, *Complaint*, 47–49:
>And as me thoght, that the nyghtyngale
>Wyth so grete myght her voys gan out[e] wrest,
>Ryght as her hert for love wolde brest,

and note to these lines.

l. 76. Among] See note to l. 61.

l. 77. I think we must assume a pause after 'advert,' meaning: 'then thou must say,' or 'then thou wilt understand.'

advert] *Kk.* i, fol. 196 a:
>Man, call to mynde // & mekely do aduerte.

M. P. 137: Lat hym adverte and have inspeccioun,
>What ther befyl in Awstynes tyme.

Ibid. 139: Awstyn was sent, who that liste adverte.
Ibid. 250: O blissed Ihesu! and goodly do advert.

Lydgate's *Vertue of the Masse*, MS. Harl. 2254, f. 182 b:
>Interpretacioun · who wisely can aduerte
>The offeratory · is named of offeryng.

(Quoted from E. E. T. S. 71, p. 233.)

Pilgr. 1637, 1638:
>Which thing, whan thow dost aduerte,
>Yt shall nesshe ful wel thyn herte.

Ibid. 3603, 3604:
>Wher-of, whan I dide aduerte,
>I hadde gret sorwen yn myn herte.

Skeat, *Chaucer*, vii, xxiv, 150:
>B[ut] in myn inward thought I gan advert.

Compare also l. 93 of our poem.

p. 19, l. 81. both[e] two] That we are authorised to supply here a sounding 'e,' the following quotations will prove, where we find always 'bothe two' required by the metre (in the lines marked with an asterisk as an

. *Notes: Poem II. Page* 19, *lines* 82–93. 59

absolute necessity), because these lines would otherwise want a syllable.
Falls, 10 b 2 :
>He and his wife compelled both[e] two.

Ibid. 38 b 2 :
>That we algate shall dye both[e] two.

Ibid. 71 a 2 :
>Which be deceiued (I dare say) both[e] two.

Ibid. 74 a 2 :
>in my person offending both[e] two.

Ibid. 76 a 1 :
>and fro the office depriued bothe twayne.

S. of Thebes, 357 a 1 :
>As write myne aucthor, & Bochas bothe two.

Ibid. 371 b 1 :
>Through my defence, and slouthe bothe two.

Degenhart, *Horse,* *39, 348 ; *Pilgr.* *1114, 1600, 1747, 2126, 4153, 5246, *5718, 5936, *7494, *7786, 7958 ; *Rom. of the R.* 4804. Also in *Hoccleve* (E. E. T. S., E. S. 72), p. 22, l. 589 :
>Whan þat þou hast assaydë boþë two.

Ibid. p. 37, l. 1007 :
>But bothë two he nedës moot forbere.

Ibid. p. 187, l. 5174 :
>ffor she was bothë two, and syn she had.

Finally, in *Confessio Amantis* (E. E. T. S., E. S. 81, 82) I find some thirty examples of 'bothë two,' so Prologus, ll. 606, 1068 ; i, 208, 253 ; ii, 1157, 2598, 3346, 3463 ; iv, 2285, 2295. ... Compare also Spies, *Studien,* § 239.

p. 19, l. 82. *ne—nothyng*] See note to ll. 52, 53.

l. 84. Resownyth] Compare Skeat, *Chaucer,* v, notes to *C. T.,* A. 275, 307, B. 3157, C. 54, F. 517, H. 195, etc., and Flügel in *Anglia,* 24 (1901), p. 483 f.

M. P. 258 :
>Nor nouht that sownyd toward perfectioun.

Falls, 52 b 2, 53 a 1 :
>For me thought it was better to abide
>on her goodnes than thyng reherce in dede
>which might resowne again her womāhede.

Triggs, *Assembly,* 1302 :
>For nothyng may me plese that sowneth to corrupcioñ.

Chaucer's Dream, ed. by R. Morris, l. 2074 :
>And all that sownede to gentilnesse.

Hoccleve (E. E. T. S., E. S. 61), p. 76, l. 90 :
>to thyng that sovneth / in-to [hy] falshede ?

Ibid. (E. E. T. S., E. S. 72), l. 1947 :
>Write him no thyng þat sowneth in-to vice.

l. 85. Occy] See note to c. l. 90.

l. 92. alre] 'old,' as the MSS. read, is quite impossible ; it gives no sense at all. Surely it is corrupted from 'aldre' (=alre), which form survives in such expressions as : altherfirst, altherlast, altherfairest, alderbest, alderlest, alderlevest, aldermost, aldernext, etc. Compare Skeat, *Chaucer,* iii, p. 300, note to l. 298 ; also Schick, *T. G.,* note to l. 70.

l. 93. adverte] See note to l. 77.

60   *Notes: Poem II. Pages* 19, 20, *lines* 94–115.

p. 19, l. 94. starf] This verb had not at that time the narrow meaning of 'to die by hunger,' but the general sense which the German 'sterben' has still.   *M. P.* 32:
    In hope that he shal sterve withynne a while.
Compare also Skeat, *Chaucer*, i, v, 420:
    Do what hir list, to do me live or sterve.
See also note to l. 183.
l. 97. thilke] occurs Schick, *T. G.* 81, and st. 25 a 7; *G. W.* (Zupitza), 35, 4; compare Skeat, *Chaucer*, vii, xxiv, note to l. 642, and Spies, *Studien*, § 50.
l. 103. Compare *M. P.* 122:
    Lyft up the ieen of your advertence.
Ibid. 198 :   Man ! left up thyn eye to the hevene,
    And pray the Lord, which is eternal !
Ibid. 209:
    For which, ye lordys, lefit up yoer eyen blynde !
Ibid. 259 :
    Behoold, O man, left up thyn eye and see,
    What mortal peyne I suffryd for thy trespace.
Pilgr. 5317, 5318 :
    Off thys fygure that I ha told ;
    Lefft vp thyn eyen & be-hold.
Ibid. 6241, 6242 :
    Lefft vp thyn Eye, be-hold & se,
    And tak good heed now vn-to me !
Hoccleve (E. E. T. S., E. S. 61), p. 210, l. 869 :
    Lifte vp thyn yen / looke aboute & see.
Anglia, vii (1884), *Anzeiger*, p. 86, l. 51 :
    Lyfte up *your* hertly eye, behold *and* se.
Similarly *Falls*, 124 a 2 :
    See with the yen of your advertence.
Compare in our poem l. 177.
l. 106. Sle] See note to c. l. 90.
ll. 110, 111. list] See note to c. l. 9.
p. 20, l. 112. theyr] refers to ' mannes,' l. 110, which must be taken as a collective noun.   Compare C. Alphonso Smith, *A note on the concord of collectives and indefinites in English* in *Anglia* xxiii (1901), p. 242 ff. The reverse case takes place l. 147 'his '; see note to this line.
l. 115. Rose] Here and ll. 118, 120 Lydgate compares the wounds of Christ with roses ; this idea may be borrowed from Bernardus Claraevallensis.   In his *Liber de Passione Domini* we find, chap. 41, the following passage :
    Vide totum corp*us*, sicubi rosæ sanguineæ florem *non* inuenias. Inspice manu*m* una*m* & altera*m*, si florem rosæ inuenias in utraq*ue*. Inspice pede*m* & unu*m* & alter*um*.   Nu*m*quid non rosei ?   Inspice lateris aperturam : q*ui*a nec illa caret rosa, q*ua*muis ipsa subrubea sit *propter* misturam aq*ue*, q*ui*a sicut narrat euangelista. . . . O q*uam* multo numero folior*um* multiplicata & exornata est rosa tua. . . .
Compare *M. P.* 26 :
    It was the rose of the blody felde ;
    Rose of Ihericho that grue in Bedlem ;
    The fyve rosis portraid in the shelde,
    Splaid in the baner at Iherusalem.

Notes: Poem II. Page 20, lines 117–133.

> The sonne was clips and dirke in every reme,
> Whan Crist Ihesu five wellys list unclose,
> Toward Paradise, callid the reede streme,
> Of whos five woundes prynte in your herte a rose.

p. 20, l. 117. go or ride] Compare Ellis, *E. E. P.* i, p. 375, and Kittredge in *Studies and Notes in Philology and Literature* (Harvard University), 1, Boston, 1892, p. 17, No. 4.

M. P. 223: In londe wheres'ere thow goo or ryde.

E. E. T. S. 71, p. 392:
> ffor in what place / I go or ryde.

(Lydgate's *Venus-Mass*, Fairfax, 16, f. 315 a.)

Add Skeat, *Chaucer*, i, xxii, 19:
> Sith I, thunworthiest that may ryde or go.

Wülcker, *Altenglisches Lesebuch* (1874), ii, 6, p. 8, l. 4:
> We been assureth, whereso we ride or goon.

l. 127. to-Rent] See note to c. l. 256.

Kk. i, fol. 195 a:
> To ffynde þy salue // my fflesche was al to-rent.

M. P. 261:
> Behold my boody with betyng al to-rent.

l. 129. al the bloode] Compare *M. P.* 235:
> To paye our raunsoum his blood he did sheede;
> Nat a smal part, but al he did out bleede.

Kk. i, fol. 194 a:
> Pale & dedely // whan al my [*i. e.* Christ] bloode was looste.

Ibid. fol. 195 a:
> Bood in þe ffylde // tyl al my bloode was spente.

Ibid. fol. 197 a:
> My bloode al spent / by distyllacyon.

Yorkshire Writers, Rolle of Hampole, ii, p. 10, ll. 41–44:
> Swete Ihesu, lorde gode,
> For me þou scheddist al þi blode,
> Out of þi hert ran a flode
> þi modir it saw with drery mode.

Unfortunately, I have not been able to find out the origin of this fancy; the Holy Scripture *e. g.* nowhere tells us that Christ lost all His blood. Compare l. 171.

l. 133. Isaye] One of Dr. Schick's splendid conjectures, for which I am deeply indebted to him. It makes not only the construction and sense entirely clear, but is also justified by the metre, as we get a good rhyme by this emendation. That Lydgate pronounced this name I-sa-í-e also in other places, is proved by the following quotations. Steele, *Secrees*, 370, 371:
> Plente of language / with hooly Isaye,
> And lamentaciouns / expert in Ieremye.

Pilgr. 3853, 3854:
> Lych as wryteth Ysaye,
> And in hys book doth specefye.

Ibid. 7005, 7006:
> A scrypture off ysaye
> Remembryd in hys prophesye.

Compare in our poem l. 148.

Compare also Percy Society, 28: *Poems of William de Shoreham*, ed. by T. Wright, p. 133:
>Thou ert Emaus, the ryche castel,
>Thar resteth alle werye;
>Ine the restede Emanuel,
>Of wany speketh Ysaye.

Hoccleve (E. E. T. S., E. S. 72), p. 98, ll. 2708, 2709:
>As vnto vs wyttenessith ysaye,—
>He shal in heuen dwelle, & sitten hye.

Ibid. p. 162, ll. 4500, 4501:
>To suë, studien men, seith Ysaye,
>And sche þe thraldom is of Maumetrye.

It occurs in Skeat, *Chaucer*, iii, p. 16, l. 514:
>That Isaye, ne Scipioun,

where in some MSS. the reading 'Isaye' has been corrupted to 'I saye,' as in our MSS.

Compare also *M. P.* 98:
>This I saye in token of plenté,
>A braunche of vynes most gracious and meete,
>At a grete fest hym thought he dide se.

The reverse case we find *York Plays*, ed. by Lucy Toulmin Smith, Oxford, 1885, p. 268, l. 375:
>Prophete ysaie to be oute of debate.

This line was emended by Holthausen, *Anglia*, 21 (1899), p. 448, as follows:
>Prophete! y saie to þe oute of debate.

p. 20, l. 135. Bosra] Compare Degenhart, *Hors*, note to l. 317. Add the following quotation, *Kk.* i, fol. 198 a:
>Royal banerys / vnrolled of the kyng,
>Towarde his Batayle, in Bosra steyned Reede.

See also *Anglia*, 15 (1893), p. 199, note to ll. 443, 448.

ll. 137, 138. This is] = 'This'; compare Schick, *T. G.*, note to l. 496; ten Brink, § 271; *Falls*, 213 b 1:
>This is very sooth, where is diuision.

Pilgr. 2064, 2065:
>Wi*th*-outë me, thys no lesyng,
>Ye shal ha no conclusyon.

M. P. 240:
>Or I passe hens, this hoolly myn entent,
>To make Ihesu to be cheef surveyour.

Rom. of the R. 3547, 3548:
>To stonde forth in such duresse,
>This crueltee and wikkednesse.

Ibid. 6056, 6057:
>With Abstinence, his dere lemman;
>This our accord and our wil now.

Chaucer's Dream, ed. R. Morris, 208:
>'Madame,' (quod I) 'this all and some.

Morrill, *Speculum*, 149, 150:
>Þis wonder of many sinful men,
>Þat þinkeþ it were muche for hem.

Notes: Poem II. Pages 20, 21, *lines* 139–159. 63

p. 20, l. 139. consistorye] = the συνέδριον of the Jews. Matt. xxvi, 59: Οἱ δὲ ἀρχιερεῖς καὶ τὸ συνέδριον ὅλον ἐζήτουν ψευδομαρτυρίαν κατὰ τοῦ Ἰησοῦ.
Kk. i, fol. 195 a:
  Stoode a-ffore Beschope / þer ffonde I no respyte
  Smytten bi þer mynystris / in þe consistorie.

p. 21, l. 141. stoole] Compare the following lines from Lydgate's *Vertue of the Masse*, MS. Harl. 2251, fol. 181:
  The stole also strecchyng on lengthe
  Is of doctours · saithe the angels doctryne,
  Amonge heretiks · to stonde in strengthe
  Fro cristes lawe · neuer to declyne.
  (Quoted from E. E. T. S. 71, p. 167.)

l. 144. can] See note to c. l. 54.
l. 145. delude] Schleich, *Fabula*, 581, and note to this word, p. 83.
l. 147. Makyng his fynaunce] = recompense, *Falls*, 70 b 1:
  For no power whan al that wer doo
  thou shouldest fayle to make thy finaunce
  Both destitute of good and of substaunce.

Triggs, *Assembly*, 1241, 1242:
  .... & then shalt thow know
  What shalbe thy finaunce; .....

See also note to these lines. Similarly, *Kk.* i, fol. 194 b:
  To make asseth // for thi transgression.

Compare Mätzner and Stratmann.
first his] refers to 'mankynd,' l. 146 = 'fynaunce for them.' Compare note to l. 112.

st. 22. Compare the following short poem from *Political, Religious, and Love Poems*, ed. by F. J. Furnivall (E. E. T. S. 15), p. 231:
  Wat is he þis þat comet so brith
  Wit blodi cloþes al be-dith?
  respondentes superiores dixerunt
  " He is boþe god and man:
  swilc ne sawe neuere nan.
  for adamis sinne he suffrede ded.
  & þerfore is his robe so red."

l. 148. Isaye] See note to l. 133.
renomed] *M. P.* 47: Famous poetis of antyquyté,
  In Grece and Troye renomed of prudence.

Falls, 20 a 1:   so renowmed in actes marciall.
Ibid. 32 a 1:   Ful renoumed in armes and science.
Ibid. 33 b 2:   most renoumed of riches and treasures.
Ibid. 89 a 2:   So renoumed, so famous in manhed.
Pilgr. 5965:   So renomyd & flourynge in glorye.

l. 152. quayers] I could not find out anything about this word; perhaps it is corrupted for 'grapes'? Compare *Yorkshire Writers, Rolle of Hampole*, ii, p. 50, l. 3, f. b.:
  for as þo pressure presses þo grapis ...

l. 153. With regard to the metre, we prefer the reading of A., and omit the article between 'and' and 'white.'

ll. 156, 158. gan] See note to c., l. 54.
l. 158. it] See note to l. 7.
l. 159. passyng grete] Very common in Lydgate's writings: *M. P.* 7,

185, 187, 217, 244, 245, etc.; *S. of Thebes*, 359 b 2, 362 a 1, 369 a 2; *Falls*, 26 b 1, 198 a 2, etc.
 p. 21, l. 161. Iourney] *i. e.* his death. Compare *Hoccleve* (E. E. T. S., E. S. 72), p. 1, ll. 1, 2:
   Honured be thu, blisfull lord a-bove,
   That vowchidsaffë this iourny to take.
 ll. 162–165. *Kk.* i, fol. 196 a:
   A swerde of sorewe // schoolde perce to þe herte
   Off my Moder // þat called is marie
   Stoode with Seynt Iohn // swouned at Caluarie
   Vnder my Croose // for feblenes fyll downe.
 M. P. 262: See my disciplis how they ha me forsake,
   And fro me fled almoost everychon,
   See how thei sleepte and list nat with me wake,
   Of mortal dreed they lefft me al allon,
   Except my moodir and my cosyn Seyn Iohn,
   My deth compleynyng in moost doolful wise,
   See fro my cros they wolde nevir gon.
 l. 166. tee] 'rend,' as both the MSS. read here, and 'wend,' the reading of A. in l. 165 instead of 'flee,' are evidently corrections of the scribes, whereas the original MS. had, no doubt, pure rhymes. Our alteration into 'tee,' O.E. 'téon,' is surely justified.
 p. 22, l. 170. disconsolate] To the quotations in Stratmann-Bradley, Mätzner, and Schleich, *Fabula* (l. 550), add:
 M. P. 205: Reste and refuge to folk disconsolat.
 Voss Gg. 9, fol. 67 a:
   Folk disconsolat to beren vp & conforth.
 Steele, *Secrees*, 390:
   Disconsolat / in trybulacyoun.
 Rom. of the R. 3168, 3169:
   And I al sole, disconsolate,
   Was left aloon in peyne and thought.
 l. 171. al my bloode] See note to l. 129.
 l. 172. neuer none] See note to ll. 52, 53.
 l. 177. See note to l. 103.
 l. 179. *M. P.* 48:
   Modyr of Ihesu, myrour of chastyté,
   In woord nor thouht that nevere dyd offence.
 l. 183. surfete] A similar case to 'starf,' l. 94, note. This word had, in Lydgate's time, not yet the restricted meaning of the modern 'surfeit' = 'excess in eating or drinking,' but means simply: 'excess,' then 'sin.' Compare e. g. *M. P.* 145, 150, 163, 174, etc.
 l. 185. apalle] *M. P.* 241:
   Lust appallyd, th'experience is cowthe.
 Ibid. 244: Shuld nevir discresen nor appalle.
 Skeat, *Chaucer*, vii, x, 46:
   Licour ayein languor, palled that may not be.
 Ibid. vii, xxii, 15:
   Meulx un: in herte, which never shal apal.
 l. 186. als blyve] See note to c. l. 219. I cite here some few of the hundreds of occurrences of these words.
 M. P. 149: Moost repentaunt for-sook the world as blyve.

Flour of Curtesye, 248 b 2 :
  Of her, that I shal to you as blyue.
S. of Thebes (Skeat), 1173 :
  Hem euerychoon, Tydeus, as blyve
Pilgr. 5763 : Par caas thow founde ther-in as blyue.
Falls, 63 a 1 : he bad his squier take his sweorde as blyue.
Skeat, *Chaucer*, i, iii, 248 :
  And here on warde, right now, as blyve.
Ibid. 1277 : As helpe me god, I was as blyve.
R. of the Rose, 706, 707 :
  And of that gardin eek as blyve
  I wol you tellen after this.
Ibid. 992 : But though I telle not as blyve.
Ibid. 2799 : Than Swete-Thought shal come, as blyve.
Skeat, *Chaucer*, vii, xxiv, 161, 404, 1441.
In our poem compare ll. 368, 371.
Hoccleve (E. E. T. S., E. S. 72), p. xl, l. 125 :
  Come of, come [of], and slee me here, as blyff.
Ibid. p. 2, l. 36 :
  For right as blyvë ran it in my thought.
Ibid. p. 19, ll. 503, 504 :
  But I suppose he schal resorte as blyue,
  ffor verray needë wol vs ther-to dryue.
Ibid. ll. 608, 1265, 1411, 1710, 1830, 2281, 2681, 2858, 3038, 3106, 3239, 3260, 3277, 3290, 4412, 4668, 4878.
Ibid. (E. E. T. S., E. S. 61), p. 4, l. 125 ; p. 117, l. 204 ; p. 145, l. 142 ; p. 152, l. 339 ; p. 153, l. 385 ; p. 156, l. 461 ; p. 167, l. 761 ; p. 202, l. 653 ; p. 219, l. 109 ; p. 221, l. 162 ; p. 223, l. 210 ; p. 239, l. 661.
Confessio Amantis (E. E. T. S., E. S. 81, 82), iv, 1854 ; v, 3318, 3520 ; viii, 1140.

p. 22, l. 194. *Falls*, 74 a 2 :
  my spousaile broke & my good[ë] name
  for euer disclaundred that whilom shone full shene.
p. 23, l. 201. *Falls*, 91 b 2 :
  Theyr poynant poyson is so penetrable.
l. 214. *Rom. of the R.* 4081–4083 :
  Lever I hadde, with swerdis tweyne
  Thurgh-out myn herte, in every veyne
  Perced to be, ...
l. 224. Triacle] Compare Triggs, *Assembly*, note to l. 12. We add the following quotations : Schleich, *Fabula*, 446, 447 (see also p. 146) :
  His freend to hym abrochyd hath the tonne
  Of freendly triacle ; . . . .
Falls, 87 b 2 : that men with sufferaunce tempre their triacle.
Pilgr. 67, 68 : A-geyne whas strokë, helpeth no medycyne,
  Salue, tryacle / but grace only dyvyne.
Ibid. 7719 : No tryacle may the venym saue.
Kk. i, fol. 196 b :
  My blood / beste triacle / for þy transegression.
Skeat, *Chaucer*, iv, *C. T.*, C. 314 :
  By corpus bones! but I have triacle.

Notes: Poem II. Page 23, line 225.

Chaucer's Dream, ed. by R. Morris, 1901, 1902:
>And said, it was some great miracle,
>Or medicine fine more than triacle.

William Caxton, *Dialogues in French and English*, ed. by Henry Bradley (E. E. T. S., E. S. 79).
11/30/2 : Who of thise wormes shall be byten
>He must have triacle;
>Yf not that, he shall deye.

31/38 : And a triacle boxe.

Ayenbite, ed. by R. Morris (E. E. T. S. 23), p. 16, 17 :
Vor-zoþe / he is ine grat peril / to huam / alle triacle / went in to nenym.

Ibid. p. 144 : þet is propreliche a dyau / and a triacle a-ye alle kuendnesse.

Percy Society, iv (1842): *Specimens of Lyric Poetry*, edited by Thomas Wright, p. 9 :
>Tryacle, tresbien tryée,
>n'est poynt si fyn en sa termyne.

p. 26 :
>Muge he is ant mondrake, th[r]ouh miht of the mone,
>Trewe triacle y-told with tonges in trone.

Hoccleve (E. E. T. S., E. S. 61), p. 70, ll. 109, 110 :
>Torne the crois to me, noble Princesse,
>Which vn-to euery soor is the triacle!

Ibid. p. 113, l. 93:
>sythen of myne hele / he gave me triacle.

The Poems of William Dunbar, ed. by J. Schipper, Vienna, 1894, p. 118, No. 20, ll. 25, 26 :
>. . . . . . . with furious rage,
>Quhilk may no balme, nor tryacle assuage,

Ibid. p. 273, No. 55, ll. 87, 88 :
>Gif that the tryackill cum nocht tyt
>To swage the swalme of my dispyt!

William of Palerne (ed. by Skeat, E. E. T. S., E. S. 1), p. 183, ll. 197, 198 :
>Ðer sprong neuer spicerie · so speciall in erþe,
>Ne triacle in his taste · so trie is too knowe.

Manipulus vocabulorum (E. E. T. S. 27, ed. Wheatley), col. 53, l. 44, and col. 205, l. 27.

Skeat, *P. P.*, B. i, 146 ; v. 50 ; R. ii, 151 ; C. ii, 147 (and note to this line, p. 37). Compare also the quotations in the *Century Dictionary* and *Coleridge's Dictionary*.

About the 'l' in 'triacle' compare *La Chanson de Roland*, ed. p. Gautier (Tours, 1894), p. 459, note to 'Bascle,' l. 3474.

p. 23, l. 225 ff. Compare the following lines from Lydgate's *Testament:* M. P. 263 :
>Ageyn thy pryde, behold my gret meeknesse!
>Geyn thyn envye, behold my charité!
>Geyn thy lecherye, behold my chaast clennesse!
>Geyn thy covetise, behold my poverté!

Raynouard, *Choix des poésies originales des troubadours*, ii, Paris, 1817, p. 35 (= *Boèce*, ll. 216–224) :
>Cals es la schala? de que sun li degra?
>Fait sun d'almosna e fe e caritat,

> Contra felnia sunt fait de gran bontat,
> Contra perjuri de bona feeltat,
> Contr'avaricia sun fait de largetat,
> Contra tristicia sun fait d'alegretat,
> Contra menzonga sun fait de veritat,
> Contra lucxuria sun fait de castitat,
> Contra superbia sun fait d'umilitat.

And Skeat, *Chaucer*, iv, *Parson's Tale*, §§ 23–83.

p. 24, l. 232. Here the words of Christ, who speaks always in the first person, seem to be finished and the song of the bird goes on.

l. 234. streyght out as a lyne] Very common expression in Lydgate. It occurs *M. P.* 17:

> From ether parte righte as eny lyne.

Ibid. 234 : Whos blood doun ran rihte as any lyne.
Ibid. 248 : Lat thy grace leede me rihte as lyne.
Pilgr. 1705 : The myddys ryht as any lyne.
Ibid. 3237 : Shope hym Ryght as any lyne.
Ibid. 4911 : Hih a-lofftë, ryht as lyne.
Falls, 31 a 1 : to folow his steppes right as any lyne.
S. of Thebes, 378 a 1 :
> And with the soile, made plain as any line.

S. of Thebes (Skeat), 1121 :
> Mid of his waye, riʒt as eny lyne.

Voss. Gg. 9, fol. 76 a :
> And off the font riht vp as a lyne.

Margarete, 228 :
> Whos blode ran doun right as eny lyne.

Also Skeat, *Chaucer*, vii, xx, 29 :
> In which were okës grete, streight as a lyne.

Ibid. vii, xxiv, 137 :
> Sherp and persing, smale, and streight as lyne.

Ibid. vii, xxiv, 785 :
> Her nose directed streight, and even as lyne.

Kingis Quair, st. 151, l. 4 :
> I tuke my leve :—als straught as ony lyne.

Hoccleve (E. E. T. S., E. S. 72), p. 113, l. 3134 :
> Thidir wil I goo, streght as any lyne.

Ibid. (E. E. T. S., E. S. 61), p. 204, l. 692 :
> To purgatorie y shal as streight as lyne.

l. 235. Similarly Thomas Wright, *Specimens of Lyric Poetry*, Percy Society, iv (1842), p. 70 :
> Jesu, of love soth tocknynge,
> Thin armes spredeth to mankynde.

l. 237. list] See note to c. l. 9.

l. 241. bountevous] Schick, *T. G.* 1384 :
> Prayeng to hir þat is so bounteuo[u]s.

Schleich, *Fabula*, 3 (see also p. 75) :
> Nat oonly riche, but bountevous and kynde.

Voss. Gg. 9, fol. 71 a :
> Pleynly reportyng bontivous lergesse.

Skeat, *Chaucer*, vii, xxiv, 414, 415 :
> But think that she, so bounteous and fair,
> Coud not be fals : . . . .

Hoccleve (E. E. T. S., E. S. 72), p. xlix, l. 32 :
   Of thi ful bountevous benevolence.
Herrig's Archiv f. d. Studium der neueren Sprachen, 107, p. 51, l. 8 f. b.:
   o bountevous lady semenygne off face.
Malory, *Morte d'Arthur*, ed. by Sommer, London, 1889/91, i, p. 733, ll. 6–8 :
   she hath ben . . . the moost bounteuous lady of her yeftes . . .
                         (Taken from *Halliwell's Dictionary*).
   p. 24, l. 245. ceriously] Compare Skeat, *Chaucer*, v, note to *C. T.*, B. 185, and vi, p. 42, and the following quotations : *M. P.* 28 :
   Remembre wele on olde January,
   Whiche maister Chauuceres ful seriously descryvethe.
Steele, *Secrees*, 352 :
   And I shulde / Reherse hem Ceryously.
Degenhart, *Hors*, 265, 266 :
   . . . . ye shall it find in dede,
   Ceriously who list the story rede.
Falls, 73 b 1 : Wryte her compleynt in order ceriously.
Ibid. 84 a 1 : But seriously this matter to conueye
   how he was made Duke and gouernour.
Ibid. 201 b 1 : And cereously he telleth here the guyse.
Ibid. (from Koeppel, *De casibus virorum illustrium*, p. 37, note 4):
   But setteth them in order seryously :
   Ginneth at Adam and endeth at king John,
   Their aventures reherseth by and by.
S. of Thebes, 357 b 2 :
   Not tellyng here, how the line ran
   Fro kyng to kyng, by succession
   Conueying doune, by stocke of Amphion
   Ceriously by line, ...
Pilgr. 8625, 8626 :
   Now haue I told the, by & by,
   Off thys stonys coryously.[1]
G. W. (Robinson), 281 (*Voss. Gg.* 9, fol. 23 a) :
   He tolde the kynge in ordre seryously.
G. W. (Zupitza), 39, 1 :
   They told hym firste in ordre ceryously.
Also in *George Ashby's Poems*, ed. by Mary Bateson (E. E. T. S., E. S. 76), p. 11, ll. 312, 313 :
   To kepe pacience thereyñ ioyously,
   Redyng thys tretyse forth ceryously.
State Papers, i, 299 (taken from *Halliwell's Dictionary*, also found in the *Century Dictionary*):
   Thus proceding to the letters, to shewe your Grace summarily, for rehersing everything seriously, I shal over long moleste your Grace.
l. 246. Similarly *Pilgr.* 4617, 4618 :
   To swych, he gaff hem alderlast
   Hys owne boody for cheff repast.
Degenhart, *Hors*, 319 :
   That yaf his body to man in form of brede.
   Compare ll. 246 ff. in our poem to 'The testament off Cryst Ihesu,' *Pilgr.* 4773 ff.

[1] Ceryously St.

Notes: Poem II. Pages 24, 25, *lines* 247–273.

p. 24, l. 247. Restoratif] *Falls*, 83 a 1 :
                Restoratiues and eke confeccions.
Giles, 90 :   Lyst ordeyne, for a restoratyff.
M. P. 146 :   Best restoratif next Cristes passioun.
Ibid. 38 :   Telle me alle thre, and a confortatife
               And remedye I shal make, up my life.
Besides, there occur in the *M. P.* the following similarly-formed words: 49 confortatyf, 50 laxatif, 136 prerogatif, 168 preparatif, 196 mytigatiff, etc.
Compare also Skeat, *Chaucer*, vii, x, 72 :
                Of confessours also richest donatyf.
Ibid. 74 :   Afore al women having prerogatyf.
Gower likewise uses the word, *Confessio Amantis* (E. E. T. S. 82), vi, 859.

l. 248. maunde] = the Lord's Supper ; compare Mätzner, Skeat, *P. P.*, note to B. xvi, 140, p. 379, and *Encyclopædia Britannica*, xv, p. 635 ; *Pilgr.* 4613 :
                The Grete Thursday at hys maundë.
Political, Religious, and Love Poems, ed. by F. J. Furnivall (E. E. T. S. 15), p. 126, ll. 380–383 :
                A tabulle þer ys þat men mey se
                That cryste made on his monde,
                On shereþorsday when he breke brede
                By-fore þe tyme þat he was dede.

l. 251. lauendere] I am not certain about the meaning of this word. The *New English Dictionary* gives the definition : ' a man who washes clothes, a washerman,' and quotes from *Househ. Ord.* 1483 (1790), 85, Of the whiche soape the seyde clerke spicers shalle take allowaunce in his dayly dockette by the recorde of the seide yeoman lavender. In all other cases I found cited in dictionaries (also in the interesting paper by G. Ph. Krapp in the *Modern Language Notes*, 1902, vol. xvii, No. 4, col. 204–206) the word denotes women. Of course we can translate it here as ' a man who washes linen,' then the meaning would be : Christ, with His blood, has cleared us from our sins. The passage, however, would also suggest the meaning ' expedient for washing,' which would be somewhat better, but unfortunately is not proved by any quotation.
Compare Prudentius, *Cathemerinon*, ix, 85–87 :
                O novum caede stupenda vulneris miraculum !
                Hinc cruoris fluxit unda, lympha parte ex altera :
                Lympha nempe dat lavacrum, tum corona ex sanguine est.

ll. 253, 254. This is not in accordance with the narration of the Gospel, according to which the soldiers raffled for it.
ll. 257, 258. Anacoluthon. First ' his moder ' is object, then Lydgate corrects himself and supplies it by ' the kepyng of hir.'
p. 25, l. 261. hym] See note to l. 7.
l. 271. *Yorkshire Writers, Rolle of Hampole*, ii, p. 103, ll. 15, 16 f. a.:
              from the toppe of his heed to the sole of his foot
      hole skynne they lefte none.

l. 273.. *G. W.* (Robinson), 365 :
                *Th*at streme of blode gan be his sydes rayle.
Kk. i, 196 b :
                My blody woundes / downe raylyng be þe tree.

M. P. 262: See blood and watir, by merciful plenté,
Rayle by my sides which auhte I nouhe suffise.
Ibid. 263: Attween too theevys nayled to a tre,
Railed with reed blood, they list me so disguyse.
p. 25, l. 280. Schick, *T. G.* l. 466 (and note):
To al þe goddesse aboue celestial.
Krausser, *Complaint*, l. 625:
That al the court above celestial.
l. 282. Compare *Falls*, 63 b i:
Where that vertue and hygh discrecion,
auoyded haue from them al wilfulnes.
G. W. (Robinson), l. 241:
Ffrome the to avoyde all despeyre & drede.
Steele, *Secrees*, l. 664:
Grant first our kyng / tavoyde from hym slouthe.

l. 284. myrrour] Very common in figurative sense; see Schick, *T. G.*, note to l. 294, and Schleich, *Fabula*, 384, 451, 665, and note to these lines on p. 114, where many quotations are found. I noticed it also, *M. P.* 93, 122, 126, 236; *Falls*, 2 a 2, 32 b 2; *S. of Thebes*, 361 a 1, 369 a 1; *Pilgr.* 7742; Steele, *Secrees*, 1457. Also Skeat, *Chaucer*, vii, v, 179, xvii, 457; iv, *C. T.*, B. 166; i, iii, 974. See also *Hoccleve* (E. E. T. S., E. S. 72), ll. 3202, 5328; *ibid.* (E. E. T. S., E. S. 61), p. 13, l. 160; and Morrill, *Speculum*, note to l. 505; Holland's *Buke of the Houlate*, ed. by A. Diebler, l. 970.

l. 285. Enarme] See note to c. ll. 129, 130.
l. 287. Carectes] Similarly *Pilgr.* 4844, 4845:
My wondys I geue hem alle fyve;
The grete karectys, brood & Reede.
S. of Thebes, 360 b 1:
Ere he was ware, Iocasta gan beholde
The caroctes of his woundes old.
l. 289. banner] Similarly *Kk.* i, fol. 194 b:
The scaaled ladder // vp to þe Croosse strecchyng
With vertuous Baner // putte ffyndes to þe fflyght.
Ibid. fol. 195 a:
A standart splayede // þy lord slayne in þat fygt.
Ibid. fol. 198 a:
Royal banerys / vnrolled of the kyng
Towarde his Batayle in Bosra steyned Reede.
M. P. 61: Behold the banner, victorious and royal!
Cristes crosse, a standard of most peyse.
Ibid. 143: The crucifix their baner was in deede.
Life of our Lady, ix (from *Warton-Hazlitt*, iii, p. 60):
Whan he of purple did his baner sprede
On Calvarye abroad upon the rode,
To save mankynde.
S. Edmund, ii, 726:
Of Cristis cros I sette up my baneer.

In our poem it occurs again l. 316. This idea may have been suggested to the poet by Prudentius, *Cathemerinon*, ix, 82–84:
Solve vocem mens sonoram, solve linguam mobilem,
Dic tropaeum passionis, dic triumphalem crucem,
Pange vexillum, notatis quod refulget frontibus.

p. 26, l. 296. conquest and victorye] *M. P.* 213, 214, 232.

l. 297. Here the tree seen by Daniel in his vision is explained to be the cross of our Saviour; there occurs another interpretation in the Parson's Tale, Skeat, *Chaucer*, iv, C. T. i, 126:

This tree (*i. e.* 'Penitence, that may be lykned un-to a tree,' *ibid.* 112) saugh the prophete Daniel in spirit, up-on the avision of the king Nabugodonosor, whan he conseiled him to do penitence.

l. 302. ascencyon] This reading of A. is preferable.

l. 305. his] *i. e.* Christ's blood, though there is no regular reference.

l. 308. Saül] Probably dissyllabic : Sa-ül; compare l. 318, 'Ta-ü,' and l. 327, 'Mo-ȳ-ses.' In the *Falls*, 61 a 1–63 b 2, where Saul's history is told, his name occurs frequently, and among all these quotations I did not find any line where it was not possible to read 'Saul' as a dissyllabic, but in the following three it *must* be read as a dissyllabic word:

61 a 1 :	space of thre dayes Saül had them sought.
62 a 2 :	Thus day by day Saül wayes sought.
63 b 2 :	Contrariously Saül was put downe.

Confessio Amantis (E. E. T. S., E. S. 81, 82) always uses this name as a dissyllabic, as the following quotations will show:

iv, l. 1935 :	Of king Saül also I finde.
iv, l. 1940 :	The king Saül him axeth red.
vi, l. 2384 :	Saül, which was of Juys king.
vii, l. 3821 :	Be Samuel to Saül bad.
vii, l. 3827 :	That Saül hath him desconfit.
vii, l. 3830 :	Bot Saül let it overgon.
vii, l. 3834 :	King Saül soffreth him to live.

l. 310. Moyses] Here again, as ll. 308, 318, arises the question whether, in Lydgate, this name is to be pronounced as two or three syllables. Without doubt poets used their licence of making it three or two as suited their convenience. In this very line we have an indisputable example that it is to be pronounced 'Moy-ses.' But, let us take the *Pilgr.*, where the name of the great prophet occurs very often, and we find that, here again, we may always pronounce 'Mo-ȳ-ses,' as in ll. 1394, 1473, 1653, 1892, 1899, 1972, 2247, 2269, 2283, 2329, 2831, 3014, 3577, 3908, 3979, 4566, 5056, 5092, 5098, 5193, 5228, 6174, etc., but there are also three lines where it is *absolutely* necessary to divide the name into three syllables:

1982 :	Hoom to Moyses ageyn.
1988 :	Kam a-doun to Moyses.
3236 :	That the hornyd Moyses.

M. P. 96 probably Moÿses :
    This noble duk, this prudent Moyses.

Chaucer, in all the lines cited by Skeat in the Glossary to his edition, reads 'Moy-ses.' But Gower, Skeat, *Chaucer*, vii, iv, 187 :
    For Crist is more than was Moÿses.

Confessio Amantis (E. E. T. S., E. S. 81), p. 13, l. 306 :
    Of Moïses upon the See.

Ibid. p. 447, l. 1656 :
    Til god let sende Moïses.

Ibid. p. 448, l. 1682 :
    To Moïses, that hem withdrawe.

Ibid. (E. E. T. S., E. S. 82), p. 138, l. 6967 :
    Upon the lawe of Moïses.

Ibid. p. 196, l. 1092 :
    Of Moïses on Erthe hiere.
Ibid. p. 272, l. 1475 :
    That finde I noght; and Moïses.
Ibid. p. 316, l. 3054 :
    Unto thebreus was Moïses.
A dissyllabic 'Moises' I found only :
  ibid. (E. E. T. S., E. S. 81), p. 319, l. 648 :
    As Moises thurgh his enchanting.
In l. 327 of our poem we have to read Mo-y-ses.
    p. 26, l. 315. serpentyne] See Degenhart, *Hors*, 313 (and note to this line) :
    Whiche wessh awey al venim serpentine.
Steele, *Secrees*, 673 :
    Whysperyng tounges / of taast moost serpentyn.
Falls, 86 b 1 : Women that age farced were nor horned.
    Nor their tailes were not serpentine.
Ibid. 91 b 2 : So depe fretteth their serpentine langage.
Ibid. 95 a 1 : Malice of wemen whan they be serpentine.
Hoccleve (E. E. T. S., E. S. 61), p. 236, ll. 572, 573 :
    In which this serpentyn womman was / shee
    That had him terned with false deceitis.
l. 316. banner] See note to l. 289.
vertu] has here the same meaning as Skeat, *Chaucer*, iv, *C. T.*, A. 4 :
    Of which vertu engendred is the flour.
Similarly Schleich, *Fabula*, 330, 331 :
    For, whan nature of vertu regitiff
    Thoruh malencolye is pressyd and bor down.
M. P. 16 : Wiche have vertu to curen alle langueres.
Falls, 1 b 2 : Which [*i. e.* the tree of life] vertue had ageinst al maladie.
Compare Thomas Wright, *Specimens of Lyric Poetry*, Percy Society, iv (1841), p. 3 :
    Dyamaund ne autre piere
    ne sount si fyn en lur vertu.
Compare c. l. 22.
signe and token] *M. P.* 238 :
    Tokne and signe of eternal brihtenesse.
l. 318. Tau] Compare notes to ll. 308 and 310, and the following quotations :
  Pilgr. 1387 : A sygne of Tav wych ther stood.
  ibid. 1405, 1406 :
    Wych, with the sygne of gret vertu
    Markyde manye with Tav.
  Ibid. 1483 : ffor the tav T, taken hed.
See also E. E. T. S. 71, p. 206, note 7 ; Gattinger, pp. 42 and 44 ; *Pestblätter des xv. Jahrhunderts, herausgegeben von Paul Heitz, mit einleitendem Text von W. L. Schreiber.* Strassburg, 1901 ; and *Biblia sacra vulgatae editionis. Recognita cura Augustini Arndt.* Ratisbonae, Romae et Neo Eboraci, 1901, ii, p. 867, note 6.—The reading of A., 'chayne,' is unintelligible.
    l. 319. Ezechiel] read E-ze-chi-el, as e. g. *M. P.* 214 :
    This is the fowle whiche Ezechiel.

Notes: Poem II. Pages 26, 27, lines 320–344.

> In his avisioun, saugh ful yoore agon,
> He saugh foure bestis tornyng on a whele,

or *Pilgr.* 1403 : Ezechyel, who lyst to look.

p. 26, l. 320. Skeat, *Chaucer*, vii, x, 140 :
> And of our manhode trewe tabernacle!

M. P. 10 : A tabernacle surmontyng of beauté.
Again : 11, 12.

p. 27, l. 324. hir wrath] = the wrath of God against her, *i. e.* mankind. Similarly Skeat, *Chaucer*, iii. *L. o. g. W.* l. 2365 :
> How she was served for her suster love ;

her suster love = love for her sister.

l. 325. Compare Prudentius, *Cathemerinon*, ed. Th. Obbarius (1845), v, 93–96 :
> Instar fellis aqua tristifico in lacu
> Fit ligni venia mel velut Atticum :
> Lignum est, quo sapiunt aspera dulcius,
> Nam praefixa cruci spes hominum viget.

ll. 327–329. *Pilgr.* 1653–1658 :
> Thys was that holy Moyses
> That ladde al Israel in pees
> Myddys thorgh the largë see ;
> And with hys yerdë, thys was he
> That passedë the floodys raage,
> And made hem haue good passage.

l. 327. Moyses] See note to l. 310.

l. 330. To insert 'with' before the relative pronoun seems to be the best solution of the difficulties presented by this line. The close repetition of the preposition 'with' in the original MS. may very easily have induced the scribe to omit one of them.

For another religious interpretation of the five stones of David, compare *Pilgr.* 8423 ff.

l. 332. gan] See note to c. l. 54.

l. 338. showres] applied to the passion of Christ occurs *Herrig's Archiv für das Studium der neueren Sprachen*, 106, p. 62 :
> but blessed be þat oure
> þat he suffird þat sharpe shoure.

Ibid. 101, p. 53 (Burgh) :
> . . . O pastor principall,
> Which for my love suffridest dethes showre.

(Also in T(homas) W(right), *Specimens of Old Christmas Carols*, Percy Society, iv (1841), p. 28.)

Compare *George Ashby's Poems*, ed. by Mary Bateson (E. E. T. S., E. S. 76), p. 8, ll. 241, 242 :
> Of holy vyrgyns, and seynt Iohn̄ Baptist?
> That here in thys lyfe suffred many shours.

Hoccleve (E. E. T. S., E. S. 72), p. xliii, ll. 207, 208 :
> thei to the dedës schowre
> have put him [*i. e.* Christ].

Ibid. p. 142, l. 3939 :
> Hym leuere is to suffre dethës schour.

ll. 340–3. See p. 57, l. 53.

l. 344. Even and morwe] Such formulas often occur in Lydgate;

compare *M. P.* 25 :
> The aureat dytees, that he rade and songe,
> Of Omerus in Grece, both North and South?

Ibid. 226 :   Noone the lyke by est ny west.
Schick, *T. G.*, 1147, 1148 :
> Hou he shal bene, boþ at eue & morov,
> Ful diligent to don his obseruaunce.

Falls, 3 a 2 :   And in this world both at eue and morowe.
S. of Thebes, 369 a 1 :
> Fare wel lordship, both morowe and eue.

Ibid. 377 b 1 : But yet alas, bothe euene and morowe.
Mumming at Hertford [*Anglia*, 22 (1899)], p. 368, l. 27 :
> Leorne þe traas, booþe at even and morowe.

Æsop (Sauerstein), vii, 74 :
> Pursweth the pore, both est and sowth.

Also *Sir Gowther*, ed. Breul, 295 (and note) :
> Wher ser þou travellys be northe or soth.

and Percy Society, iv, i, pp. 53, 59.
p. 27, l. 345. list] See note c. l. 9.
l. 346. Similarly *S. of Thebes*, 372 a 2 :
> And oure life here, thus taketh heed therto
> Is but an exile, and a pilgrimage.

Falls, 3 a 2 :   That liuen here in this deserte of sorowe
> in this exile of pleasaunce desolate
> And in this world . . .

Ibid. 18 b 1 : how this worlde here, is but a pilgrimage.
Voss. Gg. 9, fol. 40 b :
> That this lyff her is but a pilgrymage.

M. P. 101, 122, 123, 178, 198, 239, 252, 264, our life is compared to a 'pilgrimage'; besides *ibid.* 122 :
> How this world is a thurghefare ful of woo.

Ibid. :   In this world here is none abidyng place.
Compare also Flügel in *Anglia*, 23 (1901), p. 216 f.
l. 348. list] See note to c. l. 9.
l. 350. the Right[e] wey[e] take] *S. of Thebes* 363 b 1 :
> And to the Temple, the right[e] weye he toke.

Ibid. 365 a 1 : Into the hall, the right[e] waie he tooke.
Pilgr. 74 :   And that folk may the Ryhte weyë se.
G. W. (Robinson), 304 :
> With other poure the ryght[e] wey he toke.

Compare *Introduction*, § 5 a.
p. 28, l. 351. þat] We here follow A., because it betters the metre.
l. 353. As Lydgate, being a priest, uses the Bible "Vulgatæ Editionis," the single books are cited by their Latin names.
See also *Introduction*, § 6, and Koeppel, *De casibus virorum illustrium*, p. 49 and note 1.
l. 354. sugred notes] See note to l. 5.
l. 356. thorn] See note to l. 10.
l. 357. Armonye] See note to l. 4.
l. 358. This line was once probably added by a scribe in the margin, and then by another put into the poem as the first line of st. 52.
l. 366. Compare with this line *Spielmannsbuch, Novellen in Versen*

Notes: Poem II. Page 28, *lines* 368-378.

aus dem zwölften und dreizehnten Jahrhundert, übertragen von Wilhelm Hertz. 2. Aufl. Stuttgart, 1900, p. 440, note 6.

p. 28, l. 368. As by nature] See note to c. l. 219.

l. 371. I meane as thus] See notes to ll. c. 219 and H. 186. This same formula occurs : *M. P.* 149 :
> I meene as thus that noon heresye
> Ryse in thes dayes, . . .

Pilgr. 4195 :   I mene as thus : conceyveth al.
Falls, 67 b 1 :   I meane as thus, I haue no fresh licour.
Ibid. 70 a 2 :   I mene as thus, if there be set a lawe.
Steele, *Secrees*, 757 :
> I mene as thus / by a dyvisioun.

Voss. Gg. 9, fol. 99 b :
> I mene as thus for any froward delyt.

But also : Krausser, *Complaint*, 659 :
> I menë thus, that in al honeste.

Pilgr. 6945 :   I menë thus, thy sylff to saue.

ll. 374, 375. Degenhart, *Hors*, 306-308 :
> Born of a mayde, by grace, agayn nature,
> Whan he bi mene of his humylite
> List take the clothing of oure humanite.

M. P. 214 :   Whan the high lord toke oure humanyté.
Ibid. 215 :   . . . . . . whan Crist Ihesu was born
> Of a mayde most clene and vertuous.

Ibid. 249 :   which [*i. e.* Iesus] of mercy took our humanyté.

Morrill, *Speculum*, notes to ll. 365 and 367.

l. 378. ordeyned] Compare Holland's *Buke of the Houlate*, ed. by A. Diebler, ll. 733-735 :
> Haill, speciouss most specifeit with the spiritualis!
> Haill, ordanit or Adame, and ay to indure,
> Haill, oure hope and our help, quhen þat harme ailis!

LIST OF ABBREVIATIONS.

Æsop (Sauerstein) = P. Sauerstein, Lydgate's Æsopübersetzung in Anglia, ix (1886), pp. 1-24.

Æsop (Zupitza) = Julius Zupitza, Zu Lydgate's Isopus in Herrig's Archiv für das Studium der neueren Sprachen und Litteraturen, 85 (1890), pp. 1-28.

Confessio Amantis (E. E. T. S., E. S. 81, 82) = The English Works of John Gower. Edited by G. C. Macaulay [E. E. T. S., E. S. 81, 82]. London, 1900, 1901.

Court of Sapience = Wynken de Worde's print, 1510.

Degenhart, Hors = Degenhart, Max, Lydgate's Horse, Goose, and Sheep [Münchener Beiträge zur Romanischen und Englischen Philologie. Heft xix]. Erlangen und Leipzig, 1900.

D. N. B. = Dictionary of National Biography, edited by Leslie Stephen and Sidney Lee. London, 1885-1900.

Edmund = S. Edmund und Fremund von Lydgate in C. Horstmann, Altenglische Legenden. Neue Folge. Mit Einleitung und Anmerkungen herausgegeben. Heilbronn, 1881.

Falls = Tottel's print, 1554.

Flour of Curtesie = printed in Stowe's *Chaucer*, 1561.

Gattinger = Gattinger, E., Die Lyrik Lydgates [Wiener Beiträge zur Englischen Philologie, iv]. Wien und Leipzig, 1896.

Giles = S. Giles von Lydgate; see *Edmund*.

G. W. (Robinson) = F. N. Robinson, On two Manuscripts of Lydgate's Guy of Warwick in Studies and Notes in Philology and Literature, v. Child Memorial Volume [Harvard University]. Boston, 1896.

G. W. (Zupitza) = Julius Zupitza, Zur Literaturgeschichte des Guy von Warwick in Sitzungsberichte d. K. Akademie der Wissenschaften. Philosophisch-historische Classe, 74. Wien, 1873.

Hoccleve (E. E. T. S., E. S. 61, 72) = Hoccleve's Works. i: The Minor Poems, edited by F. J. Furnivall [E. E. T. S., E. S. 61]. London 1892. iii: The Regement of Princes, edited by F. J. Furnivall [E. E. T. S., E. S. 72]. London, 1897.

Kingis Quair = The Kingis Quair, edited by W. W. Skeat [Scottish Text Society, 1]. London, 1884.

Kk. i. = Cambridge University Library MS. Kk. i.

Krausser, Complaint = Krausser, Emil, Lydgate's Complaint of the Black Knight. Halle, 1896.

Mätzner = Mätzner, Eduard, Altenglische Sprachproben nebst einem Wörterbuche. Berlin, 1878-(1902).

Margarete = S. Margarete von Lydgate; see *Edmund*.

Morrill, Speculum = Speculum Gy de Warewyke, edited by Georgiana Lea Morrill [E. E. T. S., E. S. 75]. London, 1898.

M. P. = A Selection from the Minor Poems of Dan John Lydgate, edited by James Orchard Halliwell [Percy Society, ii]. London, 1840.

Pilgr. = The Pilgrimage of the Life of Man, Englisht by John

Lydgate, edited by F. J. Furnivall. Part i [E. E. T. S., E. S. 77]. London, 1899.
Ritson, B. P. = Ritson, Jos., Bibliographia poetica : a catalogue of English poets of the 12th–16th centuries. London, 1802.
Rom. of the R. = The Romaunt of the Rose *in* The Complete Works of Geoffrey Chaucer, edited by W. W. Skeat, i. Oxford, 1894.
Schick, T. G. = Lydgate's Temple of Glas, edited by J. Schick [E. E. T. S., E. S. 60]. London, 1891.
Schleich, Fabula = Schleich, Gustav, Lydgate's Fabula duorum mercatorum [Quellen und Forschungen zur Sprach- und Culturgeschichte der germanischen Völker, lxxxiii]. Strassburg, 1897.
Skeat, Chaucer = The Complete Works of Geoffrey Chaucer, edited by W. W. Skeat, i–vii. Oxford, 1894–1897.
Skeat, P. P. = The Vision of William concerning Piers Plowman, edited by W. W. Skeat [E. E. T. S. 28, 38, 54, 81]. London, 1867–1884.
S. of Thebes = printed in Stowe's *Chaucer*, 1561.

S. of Thebes (Skeat) = printed in Specimens of English Literature by W. W. Skeat. Oxford, 1871.
S. of Thebes (Wülcker) = printed in Altenglisches Lesebuch von P. Wülcker, ii. Halle, 1879.
Steele, Secrees = Lydgate and Burgh's Secrees of old Philisoffres, edited by Robert Steele [E. E. T. S., E. S. 66]. London, 1894.
ten Brink = Chaucers Sprache und Verskunst dargestellt von Bernhard ten Brink. Leipzig, 1884.
Triggs, Assembly = The Assembly of Gods : or The Accord of Reason and Sensuality in the Fear of Death, by John Lydgate. Edited by Oscar Lovell Triggs [E. E. T. S., E. S. 69]. London, 1896.
Voss. Gg. 9. = Manuscript of the Leiden University Library : Codex Vossius Gg. 9.
Yorkshire Writers, Rolle of Hampole = Library of Early English Writers, edited by C. Horstmann. Vol. i, ii : Yorkshire Writers. Richard Rolle of Hampole, an English Father of the Church and his Followers, i. ii. London, 1895, 1896.

GLOSSARY.

[Compare also the Notes.
C. D. = Century Dictionary; N. E. D. = New English Dictionary; Str. = Stratmann-Bradley, A Middle-English Dictionary; M. = Mätzner, Sprachproben II.]

abhominable, *adv.* abominably, 11/288.
abregge, *inf.* to abridge, 9/228.
abyt, 3. *sg. prs.* abideth, abides, 11/275.
accusours, *sb.* accusers, 20/139.
adolescens, *sb.* youth, 10/267.
adverte, *inf.* to heed, note, 19/93; advert, 2. *sg. subj. prs.* 18/77; aduerte, *sg. imp.* 23/229.
agreued, *pp.* aggrieved, 3/48.
aleys (thaleys), *sb.* alleys, 28/362.
allwey, *adv.* always, 11/275.
almesse, *sb.* alms, 24/241.
alre, *pron.* (*g. pl.*) of all, 19/92.
als, *conj.* as, 22/186.
alyght, 3. *sg. pt.* alighted, 5/96.
among, *adv.* from time to time, continually, 5/90, 18/61, 76.
apalle, *inf.* to grow feeble, 22/185.
arme, *sg. imp.* take arms, 6/129.
arn, 3. *pl. prs.* are, 27/335.
asonder, *adv.* asunder, into parts, 21/166 (see N. E. D.).
aspye, *inf.* to spy, espy, 20/135.
atteynt, *pp.* attainted, 20/138.
atweyne, *adv.* asunder, 23/212.
atwynne, *adv.* between, 9/214 (see N. E. D. *sub* atwin).
avale, *inf.* to descend, 13/339, 15/395; aualynge, *prt. prs.* 1/vi; avaled, *pp.* 11/276.
auctor, *sb.* author, 14/392.
awayte, *sb.* ambush, 12/302.
awrong, *adv.* wrongly, 18/79.
axed, *pp.* asked, 21/149.
ayeyn, *adv.* again, 9/226; ayen, *prp.* 6/130, 15/402.

barc, 3. *sg. pt.* bore, 26/290, 28/379.

bareyne, *adj.* barren, 10/245.
bawmy, *adj.* balmy, 17/39.
be, *prp.* by, 2/22, 3/55, 5/113.
beawte, *sb.* beauty, 23/204.
bemes, *sb.* beams, rays, 5/93; bemys, 14/391.
beth, *pl. imp.* be, 12/325.
betokenyth, 3. *sg. prs.* means, signifies, 18/66.
blyve, *adv.* quickly, 22/186.
boffettes, *sb.* buffets, 10/255.
boke, *sb.* book, 5/108; bokys, *pl.* 2/7.
bonched, *pp.* beaten, 23/206.
boote, *sb.* remedy, redress, 27/323.
brefly, *adv.* shortly, 1/xviii.
brid, *sb.* bird, 3/50, 4/69, 5/106, 7/178, 8/201, 11/275, 15/393, 19/86, 23/217; bryd, 5/101; bridde, 16/20, 18/71, 19/82; briddes, *g. sg.* 18/51, 76; briddis, 18/55, 59, 64.
byble, *sb.* bible, 9/238, 13/344.
bye, *inf.* to buy, 12/315, 22/182.

calde, 3. *sg. pt.* called, 3/56.
can = (be-)gan, 3. *sg. pt.* 6/136, 13/339, 15/395, 21/144; 3. *pl. pt.* 3/54, 16/19.
carectes, *sb.* characters, scars, 25/287.
cast, 1. *sg. prs.* intend, purpose, 18/52.
ceriously, *adv.* 24/245; see note to this line.
chaundelabre, *sb.* candelabrum, 26/320.
chese, *inf.* to choose, 7/166.
chiere, *sb.* countenance, 17/46.
clennesse, *sb.* cleanness, 23/227.
clennest, *superl.* cleanest, 28/375.
cleped, *pp.* called, 6/142, 8/187; clepid, 24/257.

cleue, *inf.* to cleave, 6/138.
cleyme, *inf.* to claim, 8/196.
colde, *inf.* to grow cold, 11/295; cold, 20/132.
complyne, *sb.* last service of the day in monastic establishments, 16/5.
couceyte, *sb.* notion, conception, 18/70; conceyt, 19/81.
conclude, *inf.* to confute, convince, 21/144 (see C. D. and N. E. D.).
connynge, *sb.* skill, 5/112; connyng, 7/177; konnyng, 8/180.
consistorye, *sb.* consistory, 20/139.
contynuauly, *adv.* continually, 20/116.
covetise, *sb.* covetousness, 23/226, 24/239.
cowde, 3. *sg. pt.* could, 10/271.
crym, *sb.* wrong-doing, sin (*collective sing.*), 14/369.
cure, *sb.* care, 5/117.
curious, *adj.* skilfully done, 4/76.

dampnably, *adv.* condemnably, 11/286.
daungier, *sb.* danger, 26/291.
dayerowes, *sb.* dawn, 3/54.
declyne, *inf.* to die, 8/186.
delitable, *adv.* delectably, 4/89.
delite, *sb.* delight, 13/352; *inf.* to delight, 17/37.
demed, *pp.* doomed, 14/375.
demeyned, *pp.* behaved, 11/286, 13/346.
depeynt, *pp.* depicted, stained, 20/134.
derre, *adv.* dearer, 9/221.
deseuer, *inf.* to dissever, 7/167, 10/268, 15/412.
devoyde, *inf.* to put away, 25/282.
dewe, *adj.* due, 15/405.
deyned, 3. *sg. pt.* deigned, 19/101.
dismenbre, *inf.* to dismember, 7/171; dismembre, 18/72.
dostow = doest thou, 2. *sg. prs.* 17/47, 18/75.
douteles, *adj.* doubtless, 27/326.
dresse, *imp. sg.* address, 2/1; *inf.* to direct oneself, pass through, 21/158.
dreynt, *pp.* drowned, 8/208.
dungeoun, *sb.* dungeon, habitation, dwelling-place, 17/33.
dyamaundes, *sb.* diamonds, 17/33.

eke, *conj.* also, 20/124, 135, 22/170, 28/370, 373.
enarme, *sg. imp.* arm, 25/285.
encheson, *sb.* cause, 4/61.
enchesoned, 3. *sg. pt.* caused, 4/84 (not in C. D., M., N. E. D., and Str.).
encoragyt, *pp.* encouraged, 2/11.
enprinte, *sg. imp.* imprint, impress, 6/128; enprinted, *pp.* 11/296.
entendyng, *prt. prs.* being intent, 4/64.
examynacioun, *sb.* examination, 25/263.
exite, *inf.* to excite, 9/213.
eysell, *sb.* vinegar, 14/368; eysel, 20/137, 25/265; eyselle, 22/196.

fade, *adj.* faint, poor, 8/180.
falsehede, *sb.* falsehood, 17/28; falsehed, 23/200.
felawe, *sb.* fellow, 21/156.
fer, *adv.* far, 3/51, 18/70; ferre, 28/352.
feres, *sb.* companions, 10/249.
feynt, *adj.* feigned, false, 19/80; 20/136, faint.
flesshlyhede, *sb.* fleshliness, 19/84 (see N. E. D.).
flour, *sb.* flower, 28/378; floures, *pl.* 17/40 (20/118), 28/377; flowres, 27/341.
folilye, *adv.* foolishly, 7/170.
forsoth, *adv.* in truth, 16/8.
forborn, *pp.* avoided, shunned, 7/159 (see N. E. D.).
fowlis, *sb.* fouls, 16/4.
fredam, *sb.* freedom, 20/111, 24/241.
freelte, *sb.* frailty, 13/351.
fret, *pp.* adorned, 17/34.
fyn, *sb.* fine, 16/21.
fyne, *inf.* to pay as a fine, 21/168.
fynaunce, *sb.* payment, compensation, 21/147 (see N. E. D. and Halliwell's Dictionary).

gadre, *sg. imp.* gather, 20/118, 27/341.
galantus, *sb.* lovers, 2/11; gaylauntes, 10/267.
gan, 1. *sg. pt.* began, 17/37, 21/156; 3. *sg. pt.* 2/25, 17/39, 20/120, 136, 21/158, 27/332; 3. *pl. pt.* 12/308, 16/7.
geaunt, *sb.* giant, 27/333.

Glossary. 81

gesse, 1. *sg. prs.* guess, 4/86.
geyn, *prp.* again, 23/204; geyne, 23/226; geyns, 26/317.
gilt, *sb.* guilt, 22/179; gylt, 12/321.
giltles, *adj.* guiltless, 23/216; gyltles, 8/186.
glotenye, *sb.* gluttony, 25/265; glotonye, 23/229.
grefe, *sb.* grief, 10/264; greues, *pl.* 14/376.

hede, *sb.* heed, 19/98; heede, 28/368.
hele, *sb.* health, 7/154, 12/317, 15/406.
hele, *inf.* to heal, 9/223, 12/319.
helle, *sb.* hell, 6/126; hell, 6/133, 144, 11/290, 15/400.
heng, 3. *sg. pt.* hung, 14/379.
henne, *adv.* hence, 13/335; hennys, 24/248.
herber, *sb.* herbary, orchard, 28/359.
heued, *sb.* head, 24/232.
hewe, *sb.* hue, colour, 20/121.
heyre, *sb.* heir, 25/274.
hogh, *adv.* how, 6/125, 7/178, 10/252, 258, 260, 12/307, 321, 13/345, 14/374; hough, 4/69, 7/156.
hokes, *sb.* hooks, 12/305.
hole, *adj.* whole, 25/271.
-huwed, *pp.* coloured, 16/2.
hyrt, *sb.* hurt, 7/154.

iblent, *pp.* made blind, 20/130.
ien, *sb.* eyes, 19/108, 20/130, 22/194; ie, 22/177.
ileft, *pp.* left, 23/220.
imeynt, *pp.* mixed, 20/137.
infecte, *pp.* fainted, injured, 6/143.
ioie, *sb.* joy, 7/168.
iuge, *sb.* judge, 10/254.

kalendes, *sb.* first of the month, 2/25, 3/45.
kepe, *sb.* heed, 17/41, 27/337.
knowleche, *sb.* knowledge, 1/ii.
korve, *pp.* carved, cut, 23/214.
kowthe, 3. *sg. pt.* knew, 11/273; kowde, 3. *pl. pt.* could, 19/93.
kyndely, *adv.* according to kind or nature, 3/33.
kynne, *sb.* kind, 28/369.

lad, *pp.* led, 10/253.
ladyly, *adj.* ladylike, womanly, 2/8.
. NIGHTINGALE.

lauendere, *sb.* 24/251; see note to this line.
leche, *sb.* leech, 14/376.
ledne, *sb.* speech, language, song, 16/16.
leep, 1. *sg. pt.* leapt, 4/59.
lenger, *adv.* longer, 14/391.
lest, *adv.* least, 15/407.
ley, *sg. imp.* lay (down), 9/222; leying, *prt. prs.* 12/304.
liche, *adv.* like, 19/102, 22/181.
lorne, *pp.* lost, 18/60; see note to this line.
lowde, *adv.* loudly, 12/307, 28/355.
lye, *inf.* to lie, 7/175, 9/222; lying, *prt. prs.* 12/302.
lyme, *inf.* to ensnare, 10/243.

maner, *sb.* sort, kind, 9/213, 18/70.
matutyne, *adj.* (*sb.* ?) matutinal, matutine, 8/187.
maunde, *sb.* 24/248; see note to this line.
mene, *adj.* mean, middle, moderate, 1/vi.
mescheues, *sb.* injuries, 14/369.
meueth, 3. *sg. prs.* moveth, moves, induces, 3/34; meued, *pp.* 2/22.
meynt, *pp.* mingled, mixed, 16/3, 27/347.
mischeue, *inf.* to come to harm, 6/137.
mone, *sb.* moon, 17/48.
mone, *sb.* moan, 21/157.
moralite, *sb.* moral of a tale, 18/65.
mornyng, *sb.* mourning, 4/70, 7/179.
mortall, *adj.* fatal, violent, 4/77, dying away, 7/178.
most, 3. *sg. prs.* must, 3/29.
mote, 3. *sg. subj.* must, 28/364.
myndely, *adv.* mindfully, 6/128 (not in C. D., M., or Str.).
mysfotyng, *verb. noun,* going astray, erring, 23/209.

nade = had not, 6/140.
nedes, *adv.* needs, 3/29, 7/157, 8/181.
nerre, *adv.* nearer, 9/222; nere, 26/292.
noght, *conj.* not, 9/212; nought, 17/45, 20/117.
none, *sb.* nones, 4/75, 5/105, 14/380, 386.
notheles, *adv.* nevertheless, 2/19, 4/82, 11/285.

G

82 *Glossary.*

nuwe, *adj.* new, 16/15.
nyghtyngale, *sb.* nightingale, 1/i, 2/13, 13/337, 15/393, 16/11, 19/104, 28/355; nightyngale, 2/16; nyghtingale, 3/34, 5/113.
nyltow = wilt thou not, 2. *sg. prs.* 27/337.
nys = is not, 17/25.

ocy = the call of the nightingale, 5/90, 98; occy, 16/14, 18/55, 59, 19/85, 23/217.
oones, *adv.* once, 23/213.
or, *conj.* before, 3/54, 17/41, 24/248.
originall, *adj.* 6/142; see note to this line.
oueral, *adv.* everywhere, 20/121.
ouergo, *pp.* overgone, 3/47.
ouerterved, *pp.* rolled over, turned down, 8/208; see note to this line.
ourys, *sb.* hours, 1/xi.
outragesly, *adv.* outrageously, 3/32.

paradise, *sb.* paradise, 7/150.
parde (= a common oath), 17/24.
passyng, *adv.* surpassingly, 21/159.
past, *pp.* passed, 9/239, 10/247.
pees, *sb.* peace, 27/324.
pepyll, *sb.* people, 7/152.
perse, *inf.* to pierce, 6/138; perce, 25/283; persed, 3. *sg. pt.* 14/387; *pp.* 3/52; perced, 23/212.
peyneth, 3. *sg. prs.* pains, 18/73.
plesaunce, *sb.* pleasure, 16/19.
pouerte, *sb.* poorness, 23/226.
poynaunt, *adj.* poignant, 23/201.
pressour, *sb.* press, 21/153, 26/304.
prime, *sb.* prime, 4/78, 8/199, 9/240, 10/251, 268, 11/300; pryme, 11/274.
primetens, *sb.* spring, 2/11, 23.
proygne, *inf.* to preen, 16/7.
prynses, *sb.* princess, 2/1; pryncesse, 2/3.
pvniched, *pp.* punished, 9/237.

quayere, *sb.* quire, book, 2/1.
quayers, 21/152; see note to this line.
queme, *inf.* to please, 9/231.
quert, *sb.* sound health, 6/130; see note to this line.
qwyte, *inf.* to quit, 21/154.

rayle, *inf.* to run, roll, 25/273.

redly, *adv.* readily or promptly, 3/39 (see Str., p. 493: rædi, or p. 496: hrad; C. reads: Redyly).
refreyd, *sb.* refrain, 16/14.
remord, *inf.* to cause remorse, 8/190.
renoueled, *pp.* renewed, made new again, 2/23.
replet, *adj.* quite full, 4/89.
reprefe, *sb.* reproof, 8/193; repref, 10/261; repreues, *pl.* 14/368, 373.
resownyth, 3. *sg. prs.* resounds, alludes, 19/84.
rewe, *inf.* to rue, 22/175.
rote (be ~), *sb.* 3/39; see note to this line.
ryghtwisnesse, *sb.* righteousness, 8/204.

safe, *prp.* save, 7/154; sauf, *adv.* except, 16/10.
sauacioun, *sb.* salvation, 15/406.
saugh, 3. *sg. pt.* saw, 20/134; 3. *pl. pt.* 20/125.
scripture, *sb.* writing, the Holy Scripture(?), 5/114; see note to this line.
seet, 3. *sg. pt.* sat, 5/97.
sely, *adj.* unfortunate, fatal (?), 7/151; see note to this line.
sempte, 3. *sg. pt.* seemed, 17/43.
serpentyne, *adj.* caused by a serpent, 26/315.
seseth, 3. *sg. prs.* ceases, 3/37.
seyn, *pp.* seen, 25/272.
seyng, *prt. prs.* saying, 14/388.
sheene, *adv.* beautifully, splendidly, 22/194.
showres, *sb.* conflicts, struggles, 27/338.
shright, 3. *sg. pt.* screeched, 5/103.
sixt, *sb.* sixte, 5/96, 13/359, 14/378, 380; syxt, 13/342; syxte, 14/365.
sle, *inf.* to slay, kill, 7/161; *sg. imp.* 16/20.
slough, 3. *sg. pt.* slew, 28/379.
smerte, *inf.* to be punished, 6/131.
sotell, *adj.* subtle, 6/136.
soth, *sb.* truth, 19/82.
sothfastnes, *sb.* truthfulness, 8/184.
soun, *sb.* sound, 4/66.
sounde, *inf.* to heal, 25/268.
spere, *sb.* sphere, 2/26, 5/92.
sperhed, *sb.* spear-head, 21/158.
spet, *sb.* spittle, 10/259.
spreynt, *pp.* sprinkled, 20/121.
sterede, *pp.* stirred, excited, 10/269.

Glossary. 83

sterres, *sb.* stars, 11/283; sterris, 17/38.
sterve, *inf.* to die, 14/364, 19/110; starf, 3. *sg. pt.* 19/94.
steuen, *sb.* voice, 3/42.
stoole, *sb.* stole, 21/141.
streyght, *adv.* straightway, directly, forthwith, 6/144, 8/198, 24/234.
streyneth, 3. *sg. prs.* strains, 18/73.
surfayte, *sb.* (surfeit), sin, 25/266; surfete, 22/183.
suwen, *inf.* to follow, 21/163.
syxt(e), *see* sixt.
syth, *conj.* since, 8/198; sith, 9/220, 10/246.

tabide = to abide, *inf.* 4/84.
takestow = takest thou, 2. *sg. prs.* 18/71.
tale, *sb.* 3/35; see note to this line.
tee, *inf.* to draw, 21/166.
tene, *sb.* vexation, injury, 22/193.
thaleys = the aleys; *see* aleys.
then, *conj.* than, 9/223.
thilke, *pron.* this, 19/97.
tho, *pron.* those, 7/167, 19/106; thoo, 3/33, 46, 11/279, 15/407.
thoght, *sb.* thought, 3/47; see note to this line.
thoure, *sb.* = the hour, 11/274.
thurghnayled, *pp.* nailed through, 24/240.
thurghperced, *pp.* pierced through, 23/210.
tierce, *sb.* tierce, 4/86, 11/277, 13/332, 337, 342.
to, *adv.* too, likewise, also, 13/333.
todrawe, *pp.* drawn asunder, 10/256.
toforne, *adv.* before, 18/58, 27/326; tofore, 20/125.
to-Rent, *pp.* rent to pieces, 20/127.
to-Rive, *inf.* break up, rend asunder, 27/332.
totogged, *pp.* pulled to pieces, 10/256.
towchyng, *verb. noun,* touch, 23/207.

trade, 3. *sg. pt.* trod, 21/155.
trewe, *adj.* true, 17/30; triewe, 18/69.
triacle, *sb.* antidote to poison, sovereign remedy, 23/224.
triewely, *adv.* truly, 18/56.
trone, *sb.* throne, 6/145.
trowe, 1. *sg. prs.* trust, 16/15.
tunge, *sb.* tongue, 22/198.
tyme, *sb.* musical measure, the same as 'tempo,' 4/80.

vale, *sb.* valley, 28/352.
vch, *pron.* each, 6/143, 9/236.
veray, *adj.* true, 2/24; verray, 5/117, 27/342; verey, 8/207.
versed, *pp.* related or expressed in verse, turned into verse or rhyme, 5/108.
vnclose, *inf.* to unfold, 20/113; 18/51, explain.
vndrestondyng, *verb. noun,* understanding, 19/81.
vnkyndly, *adj.* unnatural, 11/294, 301.
vntriewe, *adj.* untrue, false, 16/17; vntriew, 19/80.
voide, *inf.* to leave, 7/150; voidyng, *prt. prs.* making void, vacant, driving out, 27/322.
vpsmyte, *inf.* to raise, 17/39.
vyne, *sb.* vineyard, 21/167.

war, *adj.* aware, 10/241, 11/301, 13/360; ware, 12/325, 25/288.
werre, *sb.* war, 13/361.
weyfe, *inf.* to waive, 12/306.
wherthurgh, *adv.* by which, 27/321.
wont, *pp.* accustomed, 28/356.
wsynge, *prt. prs.* using, 12/305.

yaf, 3. *sg. pt.* gave, 4/61, 14/389.
ybought, *pp.* bought, 15/396.
yerd, *sb.* staff, rod, 27/327.
yerth, *sb.* earth, 6/123, 13/348, 14/384, 15/395.
ylyke, *adv.* alike, 4/87.

LIST OF PROPER NAMES.

Abraham, 1/xvii, 11/280.
Abyron, 13/349.
Adam, 1/xiii, 6/135, 148, 14/382.
Aprile, 3/43.
Aurora, 4/71, 6/120, 7/155.

Bokyngham, 2/4; compare § 4, type B.
Bosra, 20/135.

Calurie, 12/314; Caluarye, 26/290.
Citheron, 17/32.
Crist, 5/115, 6/140, 146, 10/252, 13/361, 20/122, 27/336, 28/364; Cryste, 1/x; Cristys, 1/xi.
Cupide, 17/25, 45.

Danyell, 26/297.
Dathan, 13/348.
Dauid, 26/307; David, 27/331.
Dede See, 11/292.

Edom, 20/134.
Eue, 6/135.
Ezechiel, 26/319.

Golye, 27/333.
Gomor, 11/291.

Iacob, 26/300.
Iesse, 28/377.
Iewes, 8/188, 10/258, 263, 12/307, 14/386, 21/166; Lewis, 24/254.

Ihesu, 13/334, 20/122, 28/364; Ihesus, 8/183, 14/366.

Iohn, 20/124; Iohn, 21/164, 24/258.
Iowrdan, 26/301.
Isaye, 20/133, 21/148.
Israel, 26/311, 27/328.
June, 16/1.

Leviathan, 26/303.
Longens, 14/385.
Lucifere, 6/126.
Lydgate, Dan Iohn, 28/colophon.

Marath, 27/325.
Maria, 1/heading; Marie, 24/257.
May, 2/25, 3/45.
Moyses, 26/310, 27/327.

Noe, 1/xvii, 8/204, 9/235, 11/279.
Phebus, 2/26, 5/92.
Pilate, 20/138; Pounce Pylat, 10/254.

Rede See, 27/329.

Salomon, 10/271.
Sathan, 10/249, 12/318, 21/144, 27/336, 28/379.
Saul, 26/308.
Sodom, 11/291.

Tau, 26/318.
Titan, 16/1.

Venus, 16/16.

Warwyk, 13/332.

The manufacturer's authorised representative in the EU for product safety is Oxford University Press España S.A. of El Parque Empresarial San Fernando de Henares, Avenida de Castilla, 2 - 28830 Madrid (www.oup.es/en or product.safety@oup.com). OUP España S.A. also acts as importer into Spain of products made by the manufacturer.
Printed and bound by CPI Group (UK) Ltd, Croydon, CR0 4YY

20/03/2026
02075337-0002